Principles
in Practice

The Principles in Practice imprint offers teachers concrete illustrations of effective classroom practices based in NCTE research briefs and policy statements. Each book discusses the research on a specific topic, links the research to an NCTE brief or policy statement, and then demonstrates how those principles come alive in practice: by showcasing actual classroom practices that demonstrate the policies in action; by talking about research in practical, teacher-friendly language; and by offering teachers possibilities for rethinking their own practices in light of the ideas presented in the books. Books within the imprint are grouped in strands, each strand focused on a significant topic of interest.

Literacies of the Disciplines Strand

Entering the Conversations: Practicing Literacy in the Disciplines (2014) Patricia Lambert Stock, Trace Schillinger, and Andrew Stock

Real-World Literacies: Disciplinary Teaching in the High School Classroom (2014) Heather Lattimer

Doing and Making Authentic Literacies (2014) Linda Denstaedt, Laura Jane Roop, and Stephen Best

Reading in Today's Classrooms Strand

Connected Reading: Teaching Adolescent Readers in a Digital World (2015) Kristen Hawley Turner and Troy Hicks

Digital Reading: What's Essential in Grades 3–8 (2015) William L. Bass II and Franki Sibberson

Teaching Reading with YA Literature: Complex Texts, Complex Lives (2016) Jennifer Buehler

Teaching English Language Learners Strand

Beyond "Teaching to the Test": Rethinking Accountability and Assessment for English Language Learners (2017) Betsy Gilliland and Shannon Pella

Community Literacies en Confianza: *Learning from Bilingual After-School Programs* (2017) Steven Alvarez

Understanding Language: Supporting ELL Students in Responsive ELA Classrooms (2017) Melinda J. McBee Orzulak

Writing across Culture and Language: Inclusive Strategies for Working with ELL Writers in the ELA Classroom (2017) Christina Ortmeier-Hooper

Students' Rights to Read and Write Strand

Adventurous Thinking: Fostering Students' Rights to Read and Write in Secondary ELA Classrooms (2019) Mollie V. Blackburn, editor

Adventurous Thinking

Fostering Students' Rights to Read and Write in Secondary ELA Classrooms

Edited by

Mollie V. Blackburn
The Ohio State University

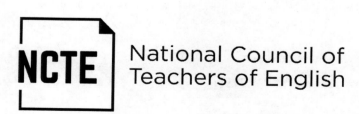

National Council of
Teachers of English

National Council of Teachers of English
1111 W. Kenyon Road, Urbana, Illinois 61801-1096
www.ncte.org

NCTE Editorial Board: Steven Bickmore, Catherine Compton-Lilly, Deborah Dean, Antero Garcia, Bruce McComiskey, Jennifer Ochoa, Staci M. Perryman-Clark, Anne Elrod Whitney, Vivian Yenika-Agbaw, Kurt Austin, Chair, ex officio, Emily Kirkpatrick, ex officio

Staff Editor: Bonny Graham
Manuscript Editor: JAS Group
Imprint Editor: Cathy Fleischer
Interior Design: Victoria Pohlmann
Cover Design: Pat Mayer
Cover Image: Grace Jensen
Chapter-opening photos:
 Chapters 1–7, supplied by authors
 Chapter 8, Anissa Photography
 Chapter 9, courtesy of Peter Haun
 Chapter 10, iStockphoto.com/CarlosDavid.org

NCTE Stock Number: 00714; eStock Number: 00721
ISBN 978-0-8141-0071-4; eISBN 978-0-8141-0072-1

It is the policy of NCTE in its journals and other publications to provide a forum for the open discussion of ideas concerning the content and the teaching of English and the language arts. Publicity accorded to any particular point of view does not imply endorsement by the Executive Committee, the Board of Directors, or the membership at large, except in announcements of policy, where such endorsement is clearly specified.

NCTE provides equal employment opportunity (EEO) to all staff members and applicants for employment without regard to race, color, religion, sex, national origin, age, physical, mental or perceived handicap/disability, sexual orientation including gender identity or expression, ancestry, genetic information, marital status, military status, unfavorable discharge from military service, pregnancy, citizenship status, personal appearance, matriculation or political affiliation, or any other protected status under applicable federal, state, and local laws.

Every effort has been made to provide current URLs and email addresses, but because of the rapidly changing nature of the web, some sites and addresses may no longer be accessible.

Library of Congress Cataloging-in-Publication Data

A catalog record of this book has been requested.

Where suspicion fills the air and holds scholars in line for fear of their jobs, there can be no exercise of the free intellect. . . . A problem can no longer be pursued with impunity to its edges. Fear stalks the classroom. The teacher is no longer a stimulant to adventurous thinking; she becomes instead a pipe line for safe and sound information. A deadening dogma takes the place of free inquiry. Instruction tends to become sterile; pursuit of knowledge is discouraged; discussion often leaves off where it should begin.

—Justice William O. Douglas
US Supreme Court: *Adler et al. v. Board of Education of the City of New York*, 1952

Contents

The Students' Right to Read

The NCTE Executive Committee reaffirmed this guideline in November 2012.

This statement was originally developed in 1981, revised April 2009 to adhere to NCTE's Policy on Involvement of People of Color, and revised again in September 2018.

Overview: The Students' Right to Read provides resources that can be used to help discuss and ensure students' free access to all texts. The genesis of the Students' Right to Read was an original Council statement, "Request for Reconsideration of a Work," prepared by the Committee on the Right to Read of the National Council of Teachers of English and revised by Ken Donelson. The current Students' Right to Read statement represents an updated second edition that builds on the work of Council members dedicated to ensuring students the freedom to choose to read any text and opposing "efforts of individuals or groups to limit the freedom of choice of others." Supported through references from text challenges and links to resources, this statement discusses the history and dangers of text censorship which highlight the breadth and significance of the Students' Right to Read. The statement then culminates in processes that can be followed with different stakeholders when students' reading rights are infringed.

The Right to Read and the Teacher of English

For many years, American schools have been pressured to restrict or deny students access to texts deemed objectionable by some individual or group. These pressures have mounted in recent years, and English teachers have no reason to believe they will diminish. The fight against censorship is a continuing series of skirmishes, not a pitched battle leading to a final victory over censorship.

We can safely make two statements about censorship: first, any text is potentially open to attack by someone, somewhere, sometime, for some reason; second, censorship is often arbitrary and irrational. For example, classics traditionally used in English classrooms have been accused of containing obscene, heretical, or subversive elements such as the following:

- Plato's *Republic*: "the book is un-Christian"
- Jules Verne's *Around the World in Eighty Days*: "very unfavorable to Mormons"
- Nathaniel Hawthorne's *The Scarlet Letter*: "a filthy book"
- Shakespeare's *Macbeth*: "too violent for children today"
- Fyodor Dostoevsky's *Crime and Punishment*: "a poor model for young people"
- Herman Melville's *Moby-Dick*: "contains homosexuality"

Modern works, even more than the classics, are criticized with terms such as "filthy," "un-American," "overly realistic," and "anti-war." Some books have been attacked merely for being "controversial," suggesting that for some people the purpose of education is not the investigation of ideas but rather the indoctrination of a certain set of beliefs and standards. Referencing multiple years of research completed by the American Library Association

The Students' Right to Read

(ALA), the following statements represent complaints typical of those made against modern works of literature:

- J. D. Salinger's *The Catcher in the Rye*: "profanity, lurid passages about sex, and statements defamatory to minorities, God, women, and the disabled"
- John Steinbeck's *The Grapes of Wrath*: "uses the name of God and Jesus in a vain and profane manner"
- Peter Parnell and Justin Richardson's *And Tango Makes Three*: "anti-ethnic, anti-family, homosexuality, religious viewpoint, unsuited to age group"
- Harper Lee's *To Kill a Mockingbird*: "promotes racial hatred, racial division, racial separation, and promotes white supremacy"
- Katherine Paterson's *Bridge to Terabithia*: "occult/Satanism, offensive language, violence"
- Toni Morrison's *The Bluest Eye*: "offensive language, sexually explicit, unsuited to age group"
- Jessica Herthel and Jazz Jennings's *I Am Jazz*: "inaccurate, homosexuality, sex education, religious viewpoint, and unsuited for age group"

Some groups and individuals have also raised objections to literature written specifically for young people. As long as novels intended for young people stayed at the intellectual and emotional level of *A Date for Marcy* or *A Touchdown for Thunderbird High*, censors could forego criticism. But many contemporary novels for adolescents focus on the real world of young people–drugs, premarital sex, alcoholism, divorce, gangs, school dropouts, racism, violence, and sensuality. English teachers willing to defend classics and modern literature must be prepared to give equally spirited defense to serious and worthwhile children's and young adult novels.

Literature about minoritized ethnic or racial groups remains "controversial" or "objectionable" to many adults. As long as groups such as African Americans, Pacific Islanders, American Indians, Asian Americans, and Latinxs "kept their proper place"—awarded them by a White society—censors rarely raised their voices. But attacks have increased in frequency as minoritized groups have refused to observe their assigned "place." Though nominally, the criticisms of literature about minoritized racial or ethnic groups have usually been directed at "bad language," "suggestive situations," "questionable literary merit," or "ungrammatical English" (usually oblique complaints about the different dialect or culture of a group), the underlying motive for some attacks has unquestionably been discriminatory. Typical of censors' criticisms of ethnic works are the following comments:

- Maya Angelou's *I Know Why the Caged Bird Sings*: "homosexuality, offensive language, racism, sexually explicit, unsuited to age group"
- Rudolfo Anaya's *Bless Me, Ultima*: "occult/Satanism, offensive language, religious viewpoint, sexually explicit, violence"
- Khaled Hosseini's *The Kite Runner*: "sexual violence, religious themes, 'may lead to terrorism'"

The Students' Right to Read

- Sherman Alexie's *The Absolutely True Diary of a Part-Time Indian*: "anti-family, cultural insensitivity, drugs/alcohol/smoking, gambling, offensive language, sex education, sexually explicit, unsuited for age group, violence, depictions of bullying"

Books are not alone in being subject to censorship. Magazines or newspapers used, recommended, or referred to in English classes have increasingly drawn the censor's fire. Few libraries would regard their periodical collection as worthwhile or representative without some or all of the following publications, but all of them have been the target of censors on occasion:

- *National Geographic*: "Nudity and sensationalism, especially in stories on barbaric foreign people."
- *Scholastic Magazine*: "Doctrines opposing the beliefs of the majority, socialistic programs; promotes racial unrest and contains very detailed geography of foreign countries, especially those inhabited by dark people."
- *National Observer*: "Right-wing trash with badly reported news."
- *New York Times*: "That thing should be outlawed after printing the Pentagon Papers and helping our country's enemies."

The immediate results of demands to censor books or periodicals vary. At times, school boards and administrators have supported and defended their teachers, their use of materials under fire, and the student's right of access to the materials. At other times, however, special committees have been formed to cull out "objectionable works" or "modern trash" or "controversial literature." Some teachers have been summarily reprimanded for assigning certain works, even to mature students. Others have been able to retain their positions only after initiating court action.

Not as sensational, but perhaps more important, are the long range effects of censoring the rights of educators and students to self-select what they read and engage with. Schools have removed texts from libraries and classrooms and curricula have been changed when English teachers have avoided using or recommending works which might make some members of the community uncomfortable or angry. Over the course of their schooling, many students are consequently "educated" in a system that is hostile to critical inquiry and dialogue. And many teachers and other school staff learn to emphasize their own sense of comfort and safety rather than their students' needs.

The problem of censorship does not derive solely from the small anti-intellectual, ultra-moral, or ultra-patriotic groups which will typically function in a society that guarantees freedom of speech and freedom of the press. The present concern is rather with the frequency and force of attacks by others, often people of good will and the best intentions, some from within the teaching profession. The National Council of Teachers of English, the National Education Association, the American Federation of Teachers, and the American Library Association, as well as the publishing industry and writers themselves agree: pressures for censorship are great throughout our society.

The material that follows is divided into two sections. The first on "The Right to Read" is addressed to parents and the community at large. The other section, "A Program of

The Students' Right to Read

Action," lists Council recommendations for establishing professional committees in every school to set up procedures for book selection, to work for community support, and to review complaints against texts. *Where suspicion fills the air and holds scholars in line for fear of their jobs, there can be no exercise of the free intellect. . . . A problem can no longer be pursued with impunity to its edges. Fear stalks the classroom. The teacher is no longer a stimulant to adventurous thinking; she [sic] becomes instead a pipe line for safe and sound information. A deadening dogma takes the place of free inquiry. Instruction tends to become sterile; pursuit of knowledge is discouraged; discussion often leaves off where it should begin.*

—Justice William O. Douglas, United States Supreme Court:
Adler v. Board of Education, 1951

The Right to Read

An open letter to our country from the National Council of Teachers of English:

The right to read, like all rights guaranteed or implied within our constitutional tradition, can be used wisely or foolishly. In many ways, education is an effort to improve the quality of choices open to all students. But to deny the freedom of choice in fear that it may be unwisely used is to destroy the freedom itself. For this reason, we respect the right of individuals to be selective in their own reading. But for the same reason, we oppose efforts of individuals or groups to limit the freedom of choice of others or to impose their own standards or tastes upon the community at large.

One of the foundations of a democratic society is the individual's right to read, and also the individual's right to freely choose what they would like to read. This right is based on an assumption that the educated possess judgment and understanding and can be trusted with the determination of their own actions. In effect, the reader is freed from the bonds of chance. The reader is not limited by birth, geographic location, or time, since reading allows meeting people, debating philosophies, and experiencing events far beyond the narrow confines of an individual's own existence.

In selecting texts to read by young people, English teachers consider the contribution each work may make to the education of the reader, its aesthetic value, its honesty, its readability for a particular group of students, and its appeal to young children and adolescents. English teachers, however, may use different texts for different purposes. The criteria for choosing a text to be read by an entire class are somewhat different from the criteria for choosing texts to be read by small groups.

For example, a teacher might select John Knowles's *A Separate Peace* for reading by an entire class, partly because the book has received wide critical recognition, partly because it is relatively short and will keep the attention of many slower readers, and partly because it has proved popular with many students of widely differing skill sets. The same teacher, faced with the responsibility of choosing or recommending books for several small groups of students, might select or recommend books as different as Nathaniel Hawthorne's *The Scarlet Letter*, Alexander Solzhenitsyn's *One Day in the Life of Ivan Denisovitch*, <u>Marjane Satrapi</u> [1]'s *Persepolis*, Malcolm X's *The Autobiography of Malcolm X*, Charles Dickens's *Great Expectations*, Carlos Bulosan's *America Is in the Heart*, or Paul Zindel's *The Pigman*, depending upon the skills and interests of the students in each group.

And the criteria for suggesting books to individuals or for recommending something worth reading for a student who casually stops by after class are different from selecting material for a class or group. As opposed to censoring, the teacher selects texts, and also helps guide students to self-select them. Selection implies that one is free to choose a text, depending upon the purpose to be achieved and the students or class in question, but a book selected this year may be ignored next year, and the reverse. Censorship implies that certain works are not open to selection, this year or any year.

Wallace Stevens once wrote, "Literature is the better part of life. To this it seems inevitably necessary to add / provided life is the better part of literature" (1957). Students and parents have the right to demand that education today keep students in touch with the reality of the world outside the classroom. Many of our best literary works ask questions as valid and significant today as when the literature first appeared, questions like "What is the nature of humanity?" "Why do people praise individuality and practice conformity?" "What do people need for a good life?" and "What is the nature of a good person?" English teachers must be free to employ books, classic or contemporary, which do not hide, or lie to the young, about the perilous but wondrous times we live in, books which talk of the fears, hopes, joys, and frustrations people experience, books about people not only as they are but as they can be. English teachers forced through the pressures of censorship to use only safe or antiseptic works are placed in the morally and intellectually untenable position of lying to their students about the nature and condition of humanity.

The teacher must exercise care to select or recommend works for class reading and group discussion. One of the most important responsibilities of the English teacher is developing rapport and respect among students. Respect for the uniqueness and potential of the individual, an important facet of the study of literature, should be emphasized in the English class. One way rapport and respect can be developed is through encouraging the students themselves to explore and engage with texts of their own selection. Also, English classes should reflect the cultural contributions of minoritized groups in the United States, just as they should acquaint students with diverse contributions by the many peoples of the world. Finally, the teacher should be prepared to support and defend their classroom and students' process in selecting and engaging with diverse texts against potential censorship and controversy.

The Threat to Education

Censorship leaves students with an inadequate and distorted picture of the ideals, values, and problems of their culture. Writers may often represent their culture, or they may stand to the side and describe and evaluate that culture. Yet partly because of censorship or the fear of censorship, many writers are ignored or inadequately represented in the public schools, and many are represented in anthologies not by their best work but by their "safest" or "least offensive" work.

The censorship pressures receiving the greatest publicity are those of small groups who protest the use of a limited number of books with some "objectionable" realistic elements, such as *Brave New World, Lord of the Flies, George, The Joy Luck Club, Catch-22, Their Eyes*

The Students' Right to Read

Were Watching God, or *A Day No Pigs Would Die*. The most obvious and immediate victims are often found among our best and most creative English teachers, those who have ventured outside the narrow boundaries of conventional texts. Ultimately, however, the real victims are the students, denied the freedom to explore ideas and pursue truth wherever and however they wish.

Great damage may be done by book committees appointed by national or local organizations to pore over anthologies, texts, library books, and paperbacks to find passages which advocate, or seem to advocate, causes or concepts or practices these organizations condemn. As a result, some publishers, sensitive to possible objections, carefully exclude sentences or selections that might conceivably offend some group, somehow, sometime, somewhere.

The Community's Responsibility

Individuals who care about the improvement of education are urged to join students, teachers, librarians, administrators, boards of education, and professional and scholarly organizations in support of the students' right to read. Widespread and informed support in and across communities can assure that

- enough residents are interested in the development and maintenance of a rigorous school system to guarantee its achievement;
- malicious gossip, ignorant rumors, internet posts, and deceptive letters to the editor will not be circulated without challenge and correction;
- news media will observe that the public sincerely desires objective reporting about education, free from slanting or editorial comment which destroys confidence in and support for schools;
- the community will not permit its resources and energies to be dissipated in conflicts created by special interest groups striving to advance their ideologies or biases; and
- faith in democratic processes will be promoted and maintained.

A Program of Action

Censorship in schools is a widespread problem. Teachers of English, librarians, and school administrators can best serve students, literature, and the profession today if they prepare now to face pressures sensibly, demonstrating on the one hand a willingness to consider the merits of any complaint and on the other the courage to defend their literacy program with intelligence and vigor. The Council therefore recommends that schools undertake the following two-step program to protect the students' right to read:

- establish a diverse committee that is representative of the local school community to consider book selection procedures and to screen complaints; and
- promote a community atmosphere in which local residents may be enlisted to support the freedom to read.

Procedures for Text Selection

Although one may defend the freedom to read without reservation as one of the hallmarks of a free society, there is no substitute for informed, professional, and qualified book selection. English teachers are typically better qualified to choose and recommend texts for their classes than persons not prepared in the field. Nevertheless, administrators have certain legal and professional responsibilities. For these reasons and as a matter of professional courtesy, they should be kept informed about the criteria and the procedures used by English teachers in selecting books and the titles of the texts used.

In each school, the English department should develop its own statement explaining why literature is taught and how books are chosen for each class. This statement should be on file with the administration before any complaints are received. The statement should also support the teacher's right to choose supplementary materials, to build a diverse classroom library, and to discuss controversial issues insofar as they are relevant. In addition, students should be allowed the right to self-select books to read from classroom and school library shelves.

Operating within such a policy, the English department should take the following steps:

- Establish a committee to support English teachers in finding exciting and challenging texts of potential value to students at a specific school. Schools without departments or small schools with a few English teachers should organize a permanent committee charged with the responsibility of alerting other teachers to new texts just published, or old texts now forgotten which might prove valuable in the literacy program. Students should be encouraged to participate in the greatest degree that their development and skill sets allow.

- Devote time at each department or grade-level meeting to reviews and comments by the above committee or plan special meetings for this purpose. Free and open discussions on texts of potential value to students would seem both reasonable and normal for any English department. Teachers should be encouraged to challenge any texts recommended or to suggest titles hitherto ignored. Require that each English teacher give a rationale for any text to be read by an entire class. Written rationales for all texts read by an entire class would serve the department well if censorship should strike. A file of rationales should serve as impressive evidence to the administration and the community that English teachers have not chosen their texts lightly or haphazardly.

- Report to the administration the texts that will be used for class reading by each English teacher.

- A procedure such as this gives each teacher the right to expect support from fellow teachers and administrators whenever someone objects to a text.

The Legal Problem

Apart from the professional and moral issues involved in censorship, there are legal matters about which NCTE cannot give advice. The Council is not a legal authority. Across the nation, moreover, conditions vary so much that no one general principle applies. In some

The Students' Right to Read

states, for example, textbooks are purchased from public funds and supplied free to students; in others, students must rent or buy their own texts.

The legal status of textbook adoption lists also varies. Some lists include only those books which must be taught and allow teachers and sometimes students the freedom to select additional titles; other lists are restrictive, containing the only books which may be required for all students.

As a part of sensible preparations for handling attacks on books, each school should ascertain what laws apply to it.

Preparing the Community

To respond to complaints about texts, every school should have a committee of teachers (and possibly students, parents, and other representatives from the local community) organized to

- inform the community about text selection procedures;
- enlist the support of residents, possibly by explaining the place of literacy and relevant texts in the educational process or by discussing at meetings of parents and other community groups the texts used at that school; and
- consider any complaints against any work. No community is so small that it lacks concerned people who care about their children and the educational program of the schools, and will support English teachers in defending books when complaints are received. Unfortunately, English teachers too often are unaware or do not seek out these people and cultivate their goodwill and support before censorship strikes.

Defending the Texts

Despite the care taken to select worthwhile texts for student reading and the qualifications of teachers selecting and recommending books, occasional objections to a work will undoubtedly be made. All texts are potentially open to criticism in one or more general areas: the treatment of ideologies, of minorities, of gender identities, of love and sex; the use of language not acceptable to some people; the type of illustrations; the private life or political affiliations of the author or the illustrator.

Some attacks are made by groups or individuals frankly hostile to free inquiry and open discussion; others are made by misinformed or misguided people who, acting on emotion or rumor, simply do not understand how the texts are to be used. Others are also made by well-intentioned and conscientious people who fear that harm will come to some segment of the community if a particular text is read or recommended.

What should be done upon receipt of a complaint?

- If the complainant telephones, listen courteously and refer them to the teacher involved. That teacher should be the first person to discuss the text with the person objecting to its use.
- If the complainant is not satisfied, invite them to file the complaint in writing, but make no commitments, admissions of guilt, or threats.

- If the complainant writes, contact the teacher involved and have the teacher call the complainant.
- For any of the situations above, the teacher is advised to be aware of local contractual and policy stipulations regarding such situations, and keep a written record of what transpired during the complaint process.

An additional option is to contact the NCTE Intellectual Freedom Center to report incidents and seek further resources (http://www2.ncte.org/resources/ncte-intellectual-freedom-center/ [2]).

Request for Reconsideration of a Text

Author _____

Paperback_____ Hardcover _____ Online _____

Title _____

Publisher (if known) _____

Website URL (if applicable) _____

Request initiated by _____

Telephone _____

Address _____

City / State / Zip _____

Complainant represents

____ (Name of individual) _____

____ (Name of organization) _____

- Have you been able to discuss this work with the teacher or librarian who ordered it or who used it?

  ___ Yes ___ No

- What do you understand to be the general purpose for using this work?

- Provide support for a unit in the curriculum?

  ___ Yes ___ No

- Provide a learning experience for the reader in one kind of literature?

  ___ Yes ___ No

- Provide opportunities for students self-selected reading experiences?

  ___ Yes ___ No

- Other _____

- Did the general purpose for the use of the work, as described by the teacher or librarian, seem a suitable one to you?

  ___ Yes ___ No

If not, please explain.

_____

_____

- What do you think is the author's general purpose for this book?

_____

_____

The Students' Right to Read

- In what ways do you think a work of this nature is not suitable for the use the teacher or librarian wishes to carry out?

  _____

  _____

- What have been students' responses to this work?
  ___ Yes ___ No
  If yes, what responses did the students make?

  _____

- Have you been able to learn what qualified reviewers or other students have written about this work?
  ___ Yes ___ No
  If yes, what are those responses?

  _____

- Would you like the teacher or librarian to give you a written summary of what qualified reviewers and other students have written about this book or film?
  ___ Yes ___ No
- Do you have negative reviews of the book?
  ___ Yes ___ No
- Where were they published?

  _____

- Would you be willing to provide summaries of their views you have collected?
  ___ Yes ___ No
- How would you like your library/school to respond to this request for reconsideration?
  _____ Do not assign/lend it to my child.
  _____ Return it to the staff selection committee/department for reevaluation.
  _____ Other–Please explain

  _____

- In its place, what work would you recommend that would convey as valuable a perspective as presented in the challenged text?

  _____

  _____

Signature _____

Date_____

At first, the English teacher should politely acknowledge the complaint and explain the established procedures. The success of much censorship depends upon frightening an unprepared school or English department into some precipitous action. A standardized procedure will take the sting from the first outburst of criticism and place the burden of proof on the objector. When the reasonable objector learns that they will be given a fair hearing through

The Students' Right to Read

following the proper channels, they are more likely to be satisfied. The idle censor, on the other hand, may well be discouraged from taking further action. A number of advantages will be provided by the form, which will

- formalize the complaint,
- indicate specifically the work in question,
- identify the complainant,
- suggest how many others support the complaint,
- require the complainant to think through objections in order to make an intelligent statement on the text and complaint (1, 2, and 3),
- cause the complainant to evaluate the work for other groups than merely the one they first had in mind (4),
- establish the familiarity of the complainant with the work (5),
- give the complainant an opportunity to consider the criticism about the work and the teacher's purpose in using the work (6, 7, and 8), and
- give the complainant an opportunity to suggest alternative actions to be taken on the work (9 and 10).

The committee reviewing complaints should be available on short notice to consider the completed "Request for Reconsideration of a Work" and to call in the complainant and the teacher involved for a conference. Members of the committee should have reevaluated the work in advance of the meeting, and the group should be prepared to explain its findings. Membership of the committee should ordinarily include an administrator, the English department chair, and at least two classroom teachers of English. But the department might consider the advisability of including members from the community and the local or state NCTE affiliate. As a matter of course, recommendations from the committee would be forwarded to the superintendent, who would in turn submit them to the board of education, the legally constituted authority in the school.

Teachers and administrators should recognize that the responsibility for selecting texts for class study lies with classroom teachers and students, and that the responsibility for reevaluating any text begins with the review committee. Both teachers and administrators should refrain from discussing the objection with the complainant, the press, or community groups. Once the complaint has been filed, the authority for handling the situation must ultimately rest with the administration and school board.

Freedom of inquiry is essential to education in a democracy. To establish conditions essential for freedom, teachers and administrators need to follow procedures similar to those recommended here. Where schools resist unreasonable pressures, the cases are seldom publicized and students continue to read works as they wish. The community that entrusts students to the care of an English teacher should also trust that teacher to exercise professional judgment in selecting or recommending texts. The English teacher can be free to teach literacy, and students can be free to read whatever they wish only if informed and vigilant groups, within the profession and without, unite in resisting unfair pressures.

The Students' Right to Read

References

American Library Association (2013, March). *Banned & Challenged Classics*. http://www.ala
.org/advocacy/bbooks/frequentlychallengedbooks/classics (Accessed June 15, 2018).

American Library Association. (2018). *Top Ten Most Challenged Books Lists*. http://www.ala
.org/advocacy/bbooks/frequentlychallengedbooks/top10#Before%201990 (Accessed July
15, 2018)

American Library Association. (2018). *Top 10 Most Challenged Books of 2017: Resources &
Graphics*. http://www.ala.org/advocacy/bbooks/NLW-Top10 (Accessed July 15, 2018)

Stevens, W. (1957, April). Adagia Part One. *Poetry*, 41–44.

The Committee on the Right to Read of the National Council of Teachers of English:

- *Edward R. Gordon, Yale University, New Jersey, Chair*
- *Martin Steinmann, University of Minnesota, Associate Chair*
- *Harold B. Allen, University of Minnesota*
- *Frank A. Doggett, D. U. Fletcher High School, Jacksonville Beach, Florida*
- *Jack Fields, Great Neck South High School, New York*
- *Graham S. Frear, St. Olaf College, Minnesota*
- *Robert Gard, Camelback High School, Phoenix, Arizona*
- *Frank Ross, Detroit Public Schools, Michigan*
- *Warren Taylor, Oberlin College, Ohio*

Statement Authors

This document was revised by an NCTE working committee comprising the following:

- Benjamin "Benji" Chang, Education University of Hong Kong, Chair
- Anna Lavergne, Houston Independent School District, Texas
- Kim Pinkerton, Texas A&M University, Commerce
- Pernille Ripp, Oregon School District, Oregon, Wisconsin
- Gabe Silveri, Cypress Fairbanks Independent School District, Houston, Texas

Permission is granted to reproduce in whole or in part the material in this publication, with proper credit to the National Council of Teachers of English. Some schools may wish to modify the statements and arrange separately for printing or duplication. In such cases, of course, it should be made clear that revised statements appear under the authorization and sponsorship of the local school or association, not NCTE.

Article printed from NCTE: **http://www2.ncte.org**

URL to article: **http://www2.ncte.org/statement/righttoreadguideline/**

URLs in this post:

[1] Marjane Satrapi: **https://en.wikipedia.org/wiki/Marjane_Satrapi**

[2] http://www2.ncte.org/resources/ncte-intellectual-freedom-center/: **http://www2.ncte.org/re-sources/ncte-intellectual-freedom-center/**

NCTE Beliefs about the Students' Right to Write

Approved by the NCTE Executive Committee, July 2014

During this era of high-stakes testing, technology-based instruction, and increased control over students' expression due to school violence, students' right to write must be protected. Censorship of writing not only stifles student voices but denies students important opportunities to grow as both writers and thinkers. Through the often messy process of writing, students develop strategies to help them come to understand lessons within the curriculum as well as how their language and ideas can be used to communicate, influence, reflect, explain, analyze, and create.

The National Council of Teachers of English believes

- The expression of ideas without fear of censorship is a fundamental right.

- Words are a powerful tool of expression, a means to clarify, explore, inquire, and learn as well as a way to record present moments for the benefit of future generations.

- Students need many opportunities to write for a variety of purposes and audiences in all classes. Teachers who regularly engage students in such writing should not be expected to read or grade all compositions.

- Teacher feedback should avoid indoctrination because of personal beliefs and should be respectful of both the writer and his/her ideas, even those with which the teacher disagrees.

- English language arts teachers are qualified to frame and assign student writing tasks, but students should, as much as possible, have choice and control over topics, forms, language, themes, and other aspects of their own writing while meeting course requirements.

- Teachers should avoid scripted writing that discourages individual creativity, voice, or expression of ideas.

- Teachers should engage students fully in a writing process that allows them the necessary freedom to formulate and evaluate ideas, develop voice, experiment with syntax and language, express creativity, elaborate on viewpoints, and refine arguments.

- Teachers should foster in students an understanding and appreciation of the responsibilities inherent in writing and publication by encouraging students to assume ownership of both the writing process and the final product.

- Teachers should explicitly teach the distinction between violent writing and violence in writing. Students should expect teachers to uphold the law in reporting all instances of violent writing.

- When writing for publication, students should be provided with high-quality writing instruction and be taught how to write material that is not obscene, libelous, or substantially disruptive of learning throughout the school.

NCTE Beliefs about the Students' Right to Write

- Administrators should work in collaboration with students who write for school publications such as school newspapers or literary magazines and, within the limits of state law or district/school policies, should avoid prior review.
- Districts should encourage the development and adoption of policies that support student writers as they learn to make choices in their writing that express their intent while still maintaining ethical and legal boundaries.

This position statement may be printed, copied, and disseminated without permission from NCTE.

Part I Introduction: Revolutionary Teaching—Ensuring Students' Rights to Read and Write

Mollie V. Blackburn

Whether students have the right to read and write is being contested in US courts. Recently, students in the Detroit Public Schools "sued state officials in federal court, arguing that the state had violated their constitutional right to learn to read by providing inadequate resources" (Balingit, 2018). In response, Judge Stephen J. Murphy III acknowledged that when a "child who could be taught to read goes untaught, the child suffers a lasting injury—and so does society," but that the Constitution does not "demand that a State affirmatively provide each child with a defined, minimum level of education by which the child can attain literacy" (Balingit, 2018). Lawyers have countered, though, arguing "the ability to read and write is key to unlocking other rights . . . that federal courts have held sacred" (Balingit,

2018). Derek Black, in Balingit's 2018 article, points out that this connection between voting and being educated dates back to before the Constitution. Ironically, the practice of tying together voting and literacy *then* was just as racist as *disentangling* them is now, since the students suing their states (California and Michigan) on the grounds of inadequate resources being provided for them to learn to read are overwhelmingly students of color (Black and Latinx). Still, NCTE asserts that literacy is a right. And this assertion, as articulated in NCTE's position statements on students' rights to read and write, is the inspiration for this book.

When I read these position statements, I am struck by this line in an earlier version of NCTE's *The Students' Right to Read*: "But youth is the age of revolt. To pretend otherwise is to ignore a reality made clear to young people and adults alike . . ." (National Council of Teachers of English, 1981/2009, p. 3). Revolt. This is not an easy word. To revolt can mean to offend, repel, and repulse. And although that is not how it is used in this statement, these meanings are there; they cannot be denied. To revolt, though, in this statement, means to defy, oppose, and resist. It is this meaning I strive to underscore.

"Youth is the age of revolt" does not mean that young people are necessarily or even potentially a part of a "Revolution," that is, "revolution thingified with that capital *R* that usually marks an icon to be shot down" (Rich, 1993, p. 237). Some might be, but that is not the focus of the book. Instead, the focus is teachers working with youth who are revolutionary, or even "potentially revolutionary" (Rich, 2001, p. 7), when revolution is understood with a "small *r* that allows for many revolutions," which Rich conceptualizes as "changes of consciousness," "invisible, unquantifiable exchanges of energy" (1993, p. 238). These many revolutions are, she describes, "parallel and converging" (1993, p. 238). The small *r* revolution allows for "continuing revolution" (1993, p. 238), or, again in Rich's words, the "long struggle for radical equality" (2001, p. 116). The young people you will read about in this book are a part of that kind of revolution inspired by their teachers.

Rich writes about artists, particularly poets, as revolutionaries, and I argue that her descriptions of artists and poets also fit teachers like those in this book. She asserts that the "revolutionary artist, the relayer of possibility . . . the revolutionary poet . . . conjures a language that is public, intimate, inviting, terrifying, and beloved" (1993, p. 250). Just as Rich's descriptions of artists suit the teachers in this book, so too does her description of art suit their practice with students:

> Revolutionary art dwells, by its nature, on edges. This is its power: the tension between subject and means, between the *is* and what can be. Edges between ruin and celebration. Naming and mourning damage, keeping pain vocal so it cannot be normalized and acceptable. Yet, through that burning gauze in a poem which flickers over words of images, through the energy of desire, summoning a different reality. (Rich, 1993, p. 242)

The teachers in this book are, in my estimation, revolutionary artists, and their teaching is revolutionary art.

And central to their revolutionary art, like the revolutionary poets that Rich describes, are words—written, read, as well as spoken. We, and they, know that in writing, we can come to understand injustices with more nuance and complexity, with more depth, when what we are writing about are issues of equity and diversity. We know that in reading, we come to understand injustices from a wider range of perspectives, or with more breadth, when what we are reading represents people, places, and circumstances that complement our own, sometimes by informing that which we already know, other times by challenging us to know more about others, and often both of these simultaneously. And all of this is understood better in the conversation with others. This demands that the youthful revolutionaries and potential revolutionaries write, read, and talk with sophistication, compassion, and strength. So, what a privilege it is not just to be the *teachers* of young people, but to be the *English language arts* (ELA) teachers of those who are in the age of revolt.

What a wonderful yet terribly tenuous privilege.

I used to teach middle and high school ELA in Los Angeles, California, and Athens, Georgia. I also engaged adolescents in writing and reading at lesbian, gay, bisexual, transgender, and queer (LGBTQ) youth centers in Philadelphia, Pennsylvania, and Columbus, Ohio. And, more recently, I had the opportunity to teach a high school LGBTQ literature course, also in Columbus. When I reflect on those experiences, I can see the faces of revolution; I can hear the voices of revolution. I remember Black and Brown students rejecting curriculum that did not include and embrace their concerns and their lives, particularly around the riots in response to the acquittal of the police officers who beat Rodney King. I recall white[1] middle-class students learning to see their privilege and the negative consequences it had on others, even their classmates, who did not share those race and class privileges (Blackburn, 1999). I remember queer kids of color dismissing teachers and schools because they couldn't seem to see that finding a place to live was more important than an assignment's due date (Blackburn, 2003). And I will never forget the ways these adolescents revolted against what they knew was wrong and the significant role of words as they wrote, read, and spoke up for themselves (Blackburn, 2002–2003).

I was also, between 2004 and 2017, part of a teacher inquiry group committed to combating homophobia and transphobia in central Ohio (Blackburn, Clark, Kenney, & Smith, 2010; Blackburn, Clark, & Schey, 2018). As a part of this group, I had the great honor of learning with teachers, most of whom were high school ELA teachers, who prepared their students, in all of their diversity, to write, read, and talk with sophistication, compassion, and strength; who prepared their students in their revolt. I learned with teachers as they guided their students in writing letters to administrators about why their schools need GSAs (known in some places as Gay Straight Alliances and in others as Gender and Sexuality Alliances); as they engaged their students in queer-inclusive texts in their ELA curriculum for LGBTQ students as well as those who had the potential to be allies, whether or not they already were; and as they prepared their students to deliver speeches at the state house to argue for enumerated language in antibullying policies. These teachers emboldened their students to write, read, and speak up for themselves and one another. They emboldened students to engage words in revolution.

Indeed, NCTE reminds us, as ELA teachers, that "words are a powerful tool of expression" (National Council of Teachers of English, 2014, p. xxi; this and all subsequent references to NCTE position statements refer to the two statements at the front of this book unless otherwise indicated), one that students not only *deserve* access to but really *require* access to if they are to participate in, contribute to, and even revolt within and against society. However, having access to the tool is not enough; students must be taught how to use the tool well. According to *NCTE Beliefs about Students' Right to Write*, subsequently referred to in this text as *SRW*, "teachers should engage students fully in a writing process that allows them the necessary freedom to formulate and evaluate ideas, develop voice, experiment with syntax and language, express creativity, elaborate on viewpoints, and refine arguments" (NCTE, 2014, p. xxi).

But even having access to the tool and knowing how to use it is inadequate if freedom to use it is restricted. Indeed, in our democratic society, the "expression of ideas without fear of censorship is a fundamental right" (NCTE, 2014, p. xxi). That is to say, students who have access to the tool of writing and the knowledge of how to use it well must also have the freedom to write about topics and ideas that may or may not align with those held by their peers, their teachers, their families, their communities, their schools, and their governments—topics and ideas related to their revolutions.

Just as writing is a tool, so too is reading, for both teachers and students. And, like writing, reading must not be censored. ELA teachers must be able to "consider the contribution each work may make to the education of the reader" (NCTE, 2018, p. xii) as they select "classic or contemporary" (NCTE, 2018, p. xiii) texts with respect to their "aesthetic value, [their] honesty, [their] readability for a particular group of students, and [their] appeal to . . . adolescents" (NCTE, 2018, p. xii). Teachers need to be able to select texts that "reflect the cultural contributions of minoritized groups in the United States, just as they should acquaint students with diverse contributions by the many peoples of the world" beyond the United States (NCTE, 2018, p. xiii). The texts ELA teachers select for their students must not "lie to the young about the perilous but wondrous times we live in"; rather, they must be "books which talk of the fears, hopes, joys, and frustrations people experience, books about people not only as they are but as they can be" (NCTE, 2018, p. xiii). But books that tell various versions of truths of these "perilous but wondrous times," truths that include "fears, hopes, joys, and frustrations," are often the books that get banned. They get censored. Such censorship puts teachers, then, in the "intellectually untenable position of lying to their students about the nature and condition of humanity" (NCTE, 2018, p. xiii). It "leaves students with an inadequate and distorted picture of the ideals, values, and problems of their culture" (NCTE, 2018, p. xiii). Censorship denies students the "freedom to explore ideas and pursue truth wherever and however they wish" (NCTE, 2018, p. xiv). According to NCTE, both teachers and students are thus the "victims" of censorship (2018, p. xiv).

Censorship, however, is not the only obstacle to students being able to use the tools of writing and reading well enough to revolt, or doing anything else they are driven to do. Consider Jonna Perrillo's blog post, "More Than the Right to Read," written in recognition of Banned Books week. In it, Perrillo offers a brief history of NCTE's role in fighting censorship. She acknowledges the important work done in the 1950s on this front but notes, too, that the effort "obscured the larger problem at hand: teachers' avoidance of anything controversial or political" and their evasion of "anything potentially contentious" (Perrillo, 2018). She asserts that

> teachers' willingness to address controversial subjects has waxed and waned over time, but it has been consistently low since the 1980s. . . . The problem, then, is not just a matter of the topics or texts we teach *but how we teach them.* (Perrillo, 2018, italics mine)

In large part, this is the driving force of this book: how we teach students to read and write "between the *is* and what can be" (Rich, 1993, p. 242).

If we believed as educators that being inclusive were enough, a list of suggested writing topics and texts would be adequate, but we know that ELA teaching is so much more than what our students read and write; it is also their (and our) thinking, talking, and listening about their reading and writing. It can be an art. It can be a revolutionary art. But it isn't always. In fact, Perrillo worries about "classroom work" that "reduce[s] potentially complex stories to easy truisms or didactic messages that compel little questioning or introspection" (2018). She knows that when students miss "out on more nuanced and complex conversations . . . they lose an opportunity to develop a more multifaceted understanding of civic life and their role in it" (Perrillo, 2018). She knows it is not the topics and the texts alone. Rather, it is the topics and the texts and the "important conversations we want them to spur" (Perrillo, 2018). It is through these conversations that Perrillo argues we can "draw students in . . . empower them to participate in ways that are rational, intelligent, productive, and democratic" (2018). And even though I do not believe that we, as teachers, *empower* students, since such a dynamic locates and maintains the power with the teachers, I do believe that teachers can engage students with writing about topics and reading texts "that might offend some," and, in doing so, we, as ELA teachers, might help "students wrestle with difference and complexity" (Perrillo, 2018).

So, NCTE's position statements on students' rights to read and write serve as a catalyst to think about how our teaching—not just curriculum, not just pedagogy, but the thinking, talking, and listening that we as ELA teachers do together with our students as they (and we) read and write—might best prepare them. How our teaching might best prepare them to engage with people—their peers, teachers, and parents—as well as to work within and against institutions such as their schools and governments. For this, we turn to accounts and reflections on teaching by teachers, by revolutionary artists.

The seven high school English teachers you are about to meet—from all across the country—understand writing and reading as tools, and they prepare students to use them well as they think, talk, and listen, as they summon a "different reality" (Rich, 1993, p. 242). To arrive at the chapters that this book comprises, I worked on several different fronts simultaneously. I drafted a list of topics that I knew teachers, whom I understand as revolutionary artists, were seeking resources for in order to explore these topics with their students. These topics are particularly pertinent today. I hope they will be less pertinent over time, but it seems to me that change happens in fits and starts and always more slowly than I hope. Even if, though, changes happen fast and some of these issues become significantly less important in the near future, the teaching practices are ones that will continue to be worthy examples. With this reality in mind, I perused the most recent years of *English Journal*, looking for high school English teachers who write about their teaching of topics in this realm. Elma Rahman, for example, wrote about being a Muslim teacher. I knew about Lane Vanderhule's efforts in her school from our collaborations in a local teacher inquiry group. I also reached out to scholars whom I knew were working with teachers doing revolutionary work. Patti Dunn introduced me to Jeff Blair; Cathy Fleischer introduced me to Tracy Anderson; Wendy Glenn introduced me to Cat Ragozzino; David Kirkland introduced me to Arianna Talebian; and Rob Petrone and Allison Wynhoff Olsen introduced me to Melissa Horner, and I'm so grateful. In reading articles and talking with people, the list I had drafted evolved, of course. Reading Rahman's article, for example, pushed me from wanting a chapter on exploring religion in high school English classes to wanting a chapter on exploring Islam, in particular, in high school English classes.

And although I very much wanted to make sure certain topics were examined, I also understood that none of these topics stood in isolation from the others or from other topics beyond the scope of this book. That is to say, Arianna Talebian's chapter on the Black Lives Matter movement is not only about Blackness, but also about nationality and gender, among many other identities. The teacher-author-artists convey this sense of intersectionality (Collins, 2009; Crenshaw, 1991) in their writing, but I also tried to underscore this in the way that I organized the chapters.

I start with Tracy Anderson's chapter on immigration, mostly because families striving to migrate to the United States during the years when this book was being written were suffering terribly due in part but not entirely to federal policies and practices. Revolutionary teachers are some of the people who can be a part of alleviating this suffering. Anderson shares her experiences teaching two journalism students as they wrote about the experiences of migrants to the United States and the devastating consequences of anti-immigration policies and practices on their lives, but also about the potential of student journalists to interrupt such consequences.

It seems to me, though, that it is hard to talk about immigration without talking about linguistic diversity, since students often migrate to the United States from places where English is not the first language young people learn, but then, when they come to the United States, most of our schools either pretend that these students know English or demand that they learn it fast. That's why Ragozzino's chapter immediately follows Anderson's. Ragozzino recognizes the importance of linguistic diversity in diverse schools and challenges teachers to enrich their high school ELA classrooms by scaffolding students' language learning while never sacrificing academic rigor and essential skills. Since many immigrant students have to negotiate tensions around religion as much as they do around their language, Rahman's chapter comes next. Rahman draws on her experience as a Muslim student and teacher in New York City schools to reflect on the dangers associated with perpetuating stereotypes with particular respect to Muslim students, and considers the importance of engaging students with autoethnography, critical literacy, and vicarious learning to counter such damaging stereotypes.

These challenges around languages and religions are not unique to immigrant students, but they are foregrounded in these first few chapters. In the following chapters, this foregrounding shifts, but just as the nonimmigrant students are not excluded from topics such as immigration, linguistic diversity, and religious diversity, neither are immigrant students excluded from the topics that follow: racial diversity, regional diversity, sexual and gender identities, and disability.

Talebian, the author of the fourth chapter, attends to just as pressing an issue as immigration. She focuses on Black and Brown people, in the United States, in relation to police brutality and the Black Lives Matter movement. Talebian begins and ends with poetic representations of classroom conversations that bookended a school year in which she committed to shaping the Black Lives Matter movement into a curriculum and pedagogy by engaging critical English education, text variation, and multimedia text production. Thus, she engages in revolutionary art in her poetry and her teaching as she facilitates her students as they write, read, and revolt. Like Talebian, Melissa Horner embraces an antiracist teaching agenda, but whereas Talebian is a person of color teaching mostly students of color in an urban school, Horner is white and Native American teaching mostly white students in a rural school. She reflects on her efforts teaching Native American literature as well as *Americanah* by Chimamanda Ngozi Adichie to teach about race and racism in the United States. In doing so, she illustrates instances wherein student discomfort, resistance, and unknowing need not be catalysts to excluding controversial texts and discussions in classrooms. I appreciate how these two chapters both fit together and don't; how they complement and challenge each other; and how they show the importance and possibility of antiracist work in revolutionary teaching done by different teachers with different students in different schools.

The final two teacher chapters represent groups about which public awareness is waxing, even as federal support is waning. There is greater freedom for LGBTQ people to live authentically and out, although this freedom seems to be coming in fits and starts and sometimes with dire consequences. There is greater inclusion for those with disabilities, due to technology, medications, inclusion programs, and the ongoing mission for students to be in the least restrictive environment. Vanderhule reflects on her experiences as an out queer teacher who includes LGBTQ-themed texts and projects, reads gay authors, and queers traditional texts with her ELA students in a midwestern suburban high school. Just as Vanderhule considers the role of minoritized gender and sexual identities in her classroom, Blair considers in his class those who encounter society's unwillingness to accommodate their physical and mental disabilities. He talks about the significance of asking students about their understandings of disabilities, including their representations in literature; how characters with disabilities are treated and how they, as readers, feel about that treatment; what lessons literature offers about disabilities; and, finally, and most significantly, how disability is a part of their lives.

When you look across the teachers' chapters, as some things get foregrounded, of course other things get backgrounded. But that does not mean, for example, that no students migrating to the United States are queer, or that no Black and Brown students struggle with society's inability to accommodate their neurological distinctions. Of course, we know that is not the case. The identities we embody are multiple and variable. Sometimes, in some situations, some identities matter more than others. And that's why none of these chapters stands alone. They stand together. And they are not everything. They are just some things, some things to get high school English teachers engaging with their students in the revolutionary arts of teaching and learning to read and write. A part of each of these chapters is a concluding list of questions crafted to challenge secondary ELA teachers to reflect on their students, to reflect on their classrooms, and to do the kinds of revolutionary teaching these seven teachers are doing with their students in their classrooms.

The book concludes with four shorter pieces that complement individual classroom teacher experiences. The first is an interview with Angie Thomas, author of *The Hate U Give* and the more recent *On the Come Up*, in which she reflects on NCTE's position statements on students' rights to read and write in relation to Starr Carter, the narrator of her first novel, and to herself as a writer. She offers teachers advice on promoting students' rights to read and write and challenges them to step out of their comfort zones on behalf of their students. The second piece is by Millie Davis, who was director of NCTE's Intellectual Freedom Center when this book was being written. She discusses how teachers can be proactive as they foster students' rights to read and write and provides resources that can support teachers in this effort. This essay is followed by my discussion of themes that run through the book in an effort to foreground what *can* be done in these "perilous but wondrous times" in which we teach and learn and live and even revolt. The book concludes with a list of annotated resources to support secondary ELA teachers in their efforts to protect and embolden students and ensure their rights to read and write.

Taken all together, it is our hope that readers and their students will uphold the teaching and learning of writing and reading as not just a right, but also an art, a revolutionary art.

Note

1. Throughout this book, when *Black* and *Brown* are used as descriptions of race, they are capitalized. When *white* is used to describe race, however, it is not. This apparent inconsistency is deliberate and following the lead of scholar Lamar L. Johnson (2018), who writes, "I have purposefully chosen to capitalize Black and other racialized language to show a radical love (see hooks, 2003) for Black and Brown people who are constantly wounded by white supremacy. In conjunction, I have chosen to disassemble white supremacy in my language by lowercasing the 'w' in white and white supremacy" (p. 121).

References

Balingit, M. (2018, August 13). Do children have a right to literacy? Attorneys are testing that question. *Washington Post*. Retrieved from https://www.washingtonpost.com

Blackburn, M. V. (1999). Studying privilege in a middle school gifted class. In J. E. Allen (Ed.), *Class actions: Teaching for social justice in elementary and middle school* (pp. 72–83).

New York, NY: Teachers College Press.

Blackburn, M. V. (2002–2003). Disrupting the (hetero)normative: Exploring literacy performances and identity work with queer youth. *Journal of Adolescent & Adult Literacy, 46*(4), 312–24.

Blackburn, M. V. (2003). Losing, finding, and making space for activism through literacy performances and identity work. *Penn GSE Perspectives on Urban Education, 2*(1). Retrieved from http://www.urbanedjournal.org

Blackburn, M. V., Clark, C. T., Kenney, L. M., & Smith, J. M. (Eds.) (2010). *Acting out!: Combating homophobia through teacher activism*. New York, NY: Teachers College Press.

Blackburn, M. V., Clark, C. T., & Schey, R. (with Penn, J. I., Johnson, C., Williams, J., Sutton, D., Swensen, K., & Vanderhule, L.). (2018). *Stepping up!: Teachers advocating for sexual and gender diversity in schools*. New York, NY: Routledge.

Collins, P. H. (2009). *Black feminist thought: Knowledge, consciousness, and the politics of empowerment* (2nd ed.). New York, NY: Routledge.

Crenshaw, K. (1991). Mapping the margins: Intersectionality, identity politics, and violence against women of color. *Stanford Law Review, 43*(6), 1241–99.

Johnson, L. L. (2018). Where do we go from here? Toward a Critical Race English Education. *Research in the Teaching of English 53*(2), 102–24.

National Council of Teachers of English (NCTE). (1981). *The students' right to read* [Position Statement, rev. 2009]. Urbana, IL: National Council of Teachers of English.

National Council of Teachers of English (NCTE). (2014, July 31). *NCTE beliefs about the students' right to write* [SRW] [Position Statement]. Retrieved from http://www2.ncte.org/statement/students-right-to-write/

National Council of Teachers of English (NCTE). (2018, October 25). *The students' right to read* [SRR] [Position Statement]. Retrieved from http://www2.ncte.org/statement/righttoreadguideline/

Perrillo, J. (2018, September 29). More than the right to read [Blog post]. Retrieved from http://www2.ncte.org/blog/2018/09/more-than-the-right-to-read-2/

Rich, A. (1993.) *What is found there: Notebooks on poetry and politics*. New York, NY: W. W. Norton.

Rich, A. (2001). *Arts of the possible: Essays and conversations*. New York, NY: W. W. Norton.

Part II
Revolutionary Artists: Teachers' Accounts and Reflections

Journalism as a Way to Foster Students' Rights to Read and Write about Immigration

Tracy Anderson

Last May, a student in the high school where I teach came into my journalism class and asked if she could make an announcement. She wondered if there was a student in the class who could cover a story about a father from another local high school who was being detained and at risk of deportation. Kyndall Flowers, a senior in the class, was at her computer working on laying out an article but raised her hand. She was busy, she said, but she always had time for important stories like this. "At first it just seemed like something that needed to be done," Kyndall said. "I saw it and jumped at it because it [the deportation] was a time-sensitive thing. I had time, so I took it." Kyndall was a few weeks away from graduating, and despite the fact that senioritis had settled in for some of her classmates, she still took her journalism seriously.

Kyndall had signed up for journalism both because she wanted to take an English class that went beyond normal essay writing and because she had been thinking about going into journalism as a form of social justice work. Although

Kyndall hoped that her writing would make a difference in the world, she also understood journalism's limits—that, in this case, journalism alone couldn't necessarily change the life circumstances of José Luis Sanchez-Ronquillo and his family, who were the focus of the story she agreed to cover. Still, she reminded herself of what journalism can do: that "journalism is just telling the story. . . . And [even] if I can't bring their family home, I [can do] everything I can to get the truth out."

Getting the truth out wasn't always easy to do. "I learned that there was a lot that I couldn't say," Kyndall explained.

> In the beginning I wasn't allowed to talk about his wife because she wasn't a citizen here, and if her name got in the story, then they were afraid ICE would come after her and try to deport her too. So I focused the story around his youngest son Charlie, who is ten years old. He is very talkative. He is very popular in his elementary school. Had a lot of friends and a lot of family behind him. I just took this really charismatic kid who had some really great stories with his father about playing soccer and playing video games, and just told that.

Kyndall first talked to Charlie at a meeting where adults were gathered to strategize about what steps to take surrounding the imminent deportation. Charlie got up in the middle of the meeting and walked to the back of the room where there was a whiteboard. He used the markers to make a rainbow. Kyndall followed him there and sat beside him. It was at that moment that she realized that her story was about Charlie, a ten-year-old boy who is an American citizen.

Charlie taught Kyndall that every story has many powerful moments embedded in them. She came to understand Charlie and his father through the vignettes that Charlie shared. "Those little tidbits when you find humanity in people who have their humanity taken away from them," Kyndall said. "Being able to tell that truth can open up a whole world for Charlie and people who don't really know that Charlie and his family do family things like play soccer and video games." Kyndall's article helped readers understand José's story through the eyes of his son, Charlie. The small details that Kyndall discovered allowed readers to better understand the immigration issue that was playing out in our community.

Kyndall explained why it was important for her to understand and tell the smaller details of Charlie's life. "I think one of the best things that someone can do is to humanize people for other people to understand them," Kyndall said.

> People have been dehumanized for such a long time, and a lot of times the only thing you see of marginalized people is their pain—and not necessarily the positive, happy familial things. So being able to open that and show the world that these people that are just like anyone else, they just have a different set of circumstances and problems, and they deserve what anyone else has.

Even after Kyndall graduated and her final grade for the course was submitted, she continued with her reporting and writing. "I want the family to know that I do not plan on stopping covering the case," Kyndall said.

> I will be there when they go to Cincinnati [to appeal to the Supreme Court]. I want to be able to follow this as far as I can. The case is so much bigger than me. It's a story that needs to be told. They deserve to have their story told. On a personal level, they deserve to have people know what is happening to them and what is going on with so many other people around this country, and that they aren't alone in this.

Kyndall believes that journalism can be a catalyst for change. When asked what advice she would give to teachers, she said, "I think teachers should teach teenagers to be critical of the world around them and do everything that they can to find the truth around them." The role of teachers, she continued, is to help students seek truth and knowledge, which is exactly what she did when she researched, reported, wrote, and edited her article about Charlie and his dad.

Why Journalism: Students' Rights to Read and Write

Although I had no experience in journalism, early in my career I found myself teaching it. I relied heavily on five workshop principles for writing—choice, time, community, audience, and instruction—that I learned in 1995 and still hold at the center of my pedagogical decisions and practice. So, as I switched from ELA to teaching journalism, I drew on those principles as well as a strategy for genre study that I learned in my undergrad methods class called 3 Is: Immersion, Inquiry, and Integration. (Later iterations of that way of thinking about genre found their way into a book by my methods teacher and a high school colleague [Fleischer & Andrew-Vaughan, 2009].) To *immerse* students in journalism, we spent time in class looking at articles: Pulitzer Prize winners, sports, news, editorials, and more. We made observations about and *inquiries* into the writing: How did the lead start? How long were the paragraphs? How many sources were there? What was the quote format? What information was included? How did the article end? We spent class periods looking at articles and deconstructing them; students came to understand the genre by being immersed in it and inquiring about the information and construction. And finally, we practiced *integration*: integrating all they had learned as they returned to their list of observations and their real-world models in order to write articles. Immersion, inquiry, and integration meant that they were never alone in the writing process, and they never started with a blank page.

Students also learned early on that an essential part of writing an article is primary research, which, in my class, always included at least one interview, but more typically three to five. Once students had completed an interview, they transcribed it and then highlighted direct quotations in one color and indirect quotations/information in another color. Thus, when students started writing any article, their page was never blank; they had their transcripts with quotations already there.

These workshop principles led students to tell stories that mattered to our community. They always chose their own topics. They had time to work on their own writing during class, and that time made it possible for me to help them as questions came up organically during their writing process. This was where we did mini-lessons about colons, semicolons, commas, and conjunctions because these budding journalists wanted to make sure their sentences were correct before the article went public.

The students had their peers and me to give them feedback before their work went public, and they later had responses from readers that came after their work went public. In other words, we always had a community of readers and writers. Students always knew that their work had a purpose in the world and that it would be read by people outside of our classroom. It was this authentic and *unknown* audience that was a critical motivator for my students' work. And this was what made my journalism class so different from other English classes I have taught, the essential component that my traditional writing workshop classroom was always missing. I would, for example, create anthologies with students and have poetry readings in the media center where we invited parents in to hear their work. Although I could argue that these *known* audiences were still valuable audiences, I also know that during my past seventeen years advising journalists, it has been that *unknown* authentic audience that has been a true motivator for the students' writing.

How does an unknown audience connect to students' rights to read and write? When we published breaking stories in our online publication, we spent class periods watching a map of the analytics. We could see how many people were reading the article and their locations. We knew how long they spent there. We knew where they jumped to next on the site. We knew the source that got them to the site. Sometimes readers responded to my journalists. Students learned quickly that their words mattered, and that they had to be sure they believed in and could support their words. Students learned the power of research and the responsibility for truth. They learned that journalism can inform people and motivate them to speak out about injustices or issues that matter to them. The right to write, in other words, is inexorably tied to the responsibility to do so.

This past year, as shown in the previous vignette and the one that follows, we saw this clearly in our classroom around immigration issues. My journalists were called on to be the ones who broke stories. They became known outside my classroom as the intelligent, meticulous, and caring people that they were. This year, more than any other year, I saw students rise up and truly give voice to the underrepresented. They used their right to write, and they made a difference.

Setting the Stage for This Kind of Journalism

One of the first lessons that I taught journalism students was about First Amendment rights. We learned about *Tinker v. Des Moines*, the landmark case that said students' rights are not shed "'at the schoolhouse gate'" (2000). And we learned about Hazelwood, a case that took away students' rights in the late 1980s and gave permission for administrators to censor work that could cause "'material and substantial disruption'" (*Tinker v. Des Moines*, 2000). However, as I explained to students, schools can still exist under the Tinker standard. Students have a right to read and write—and in the case of my classroom, they had a right to publish their work. They took 100 percent responsibility for the work that they did. They knew that if there was a question or a complaint, they would be the ones defending their words, even though, as I always told them, I would sit beside them. But we rarely had complaints, and even more rarely had meetings where students had to defend their work. However, when it has happened, students were always able to stand behind their work, pulling out their research (including transcripts and audio recordings) to support their writing, and they have been able to explain why their work was important and accurate. These students took their work seriously, and so did our community. Students knew that they could write, and that they should write, about issues that mattered most to them and our community. And they understood the responsibility that is inherent in this work, the responsibility that is connected to their rights to read and write.

A Deportation Diverted

When one of my senior student journalists, Joel Appel-Kraut, first visited the Ajin home, he came with a purpose: to write a story about the family of one of his peers. The father of three had recently been detained and was at risk of deportation. The children, ages eighteen, sixteen, and sixteen, had all been born in the United States. The deportation hearing was scheduled, but the story wasn't out in the media. Joel, a student journalist, became the one who broke the story.

As he walked into the home, he experienced the discomfort that many new journalists face. He didn't know what to expect or how to behave, for example, whether he should take his shoes off or not. But the family made room for him on the couch. They got him a glass of tea. Joel understood immediately that he had walked into a home. "It was very clear that this was a family and how much they loved each other," Joel said. This immersion in the family and their experiences helped him identify the story that was unfolding in front of him.

I didn't realize in the moment . . . I didn't really know what I had until I re-listened and transcribed it that night. That there is a real story here. I didn't understand what my role as a journalist was while I was talking to them. I was just trying to understand, which maybe is my role as a journalist.

Joel was a strong student in his English classes. But there was a difference in the writing that he did when he was writing for a teacher compared to his writing journalism for a larger community. "I was much more focused," Joel said.

> I care about school, but this is something that I was very motivated to get right. I knew that there wasn't any other option besides getting it right. It is different because with an essay for a teacher, you have a template, something you have been studying for a long time. I didn't have a whole lot to start with, and you just build it up and use quotes, which is what I love so much about it. I heard what they were trying to say and they get one chance to say it, and I have a million chances to set up that quote and in the most perfect way try to communicate what they are trying to say as clearly as possible.

While writing such an important article, Joel knew the pressure on his work. "There is no option to get it wrong," he said. "You can't misrepresent the people who allow you to step into their lives and expose them to the world." Joel spent hours transcribing, writing, and editing his article. He got the story right.

Yousef Ajin, a Kuwait-born Jordanian immigrant, came to the United States eighteen years ago. He married a woman with US citizenship, and they had four children, all of whom were US citizens. Ajin went to what he thought was a routine immigration check-in meeting, but this time he was detained and given a deportation hearing date. He was detained in a jail eighty miles from his home. His family was scared, and they needed to get their story out in the world. They were also in the unique position that everyone else in their home was a US citizen; this detail made a difference in their decision to go public with the story. Joel reported and wrote the story in one day—he had to—before Ajin's deportation hearing. Once Joel published it on our school website, the article went viral. The journalists in our class posted it on Twitter and shared it on Facebook. The superintendent shared it. The mayor shared it. Our local Ann Arbor paper picked up the story. The Detroit newspapers and radio and television stations picked up the story. Michigan Public Radio picked up the story.

Joel's story radiated through our community. "I felt respected as a student journalist," he said.

> In the world, you hear so many negative things about journalists. It made me feel less like a student and more like a journalist. It doesn't really matter how old I am; I wrote something that was worthy of someone's time and worthy of people's attention, and that transcends your age.

Before Joel's article, Ajin's story was unknown. The article brought hundreds of people to the Detroit courthouse on the day of the deportation hearing: young people who went to school with Ajin's daughters; teachers and parents from across the school district; groups of women and men who had heard about the story on the Detroit news stations; leaders of the NAACP; college students from Wayne State University. It was a diverse group of 300 people who gathered with signs and marched for hours as the hearing went on. In addition, as a result of Joel's article, hundreds of people wrote letters of support for Ajin. At a local elementary school, students, teachers, and parents gathered after school for two hours; they read Joel's article and then they started writing letters of support. While the hearing was going on, family members who were outside the courtroom quietly read stacks of letters written by students, parents, teachers, administrators, and community members.

Without Joel's article, the deportation hearing could have happened quietly and without the community's support. "First of all, it [the article] made people know," Joel said.

> That is the scariest part to me. Nobody knew. This sort of thing happens all the time and goes all the way to the trial, and they lose the trial without anybody ever knowing. Just making people know is the most important part, and that is at the core of journalism. It really is bringing information to people, but it also made people care.

Journalism has the power to bring people together, and in our age of digital media, news travels fast and networks can be quickly created. "Things going viral or getting shared around can be really powerful because you see a network of people who care," Joel said. "I got to see that network in Ann Arbor was thousands of people strong. That network still exists. The article created a network of people who cared."

From the moment that Joel entered the Ajin home, unsure whether he should take off his shoes, he was uncomfortable. He offered,

> Be comfortable being uncomfortable. That was the hardest thing for me. I second-guessed myself the entire way through for a bevy of different reasons. From the beginning to the end, I was always uncomfortable with something. Whether it was writing a story that I wasn't sure was complete or being in a room with a bunch of people I didn't know and asking them about very touchy subjects, or being in a room with ten professional reporters and being a student journalist. You have to be comfortable being uncomfortable because the uncomfortable situations are the ones that nobody else is willing to enter, and that's where journalists are important.

The Time Is Now

I realized over the past twenty years that journalism is the greatest key to authentic student writing. Intrinsically embedded in journalism are all of the great lessons that I want to teach students. I have taught them about research; primary and secondary sources; grammar lessons that they actually use in their writing; effective leads; story structures; effective persuasive techniques using ethos, pathos and logos; and more. Journalism gives students a reason to care about something outside themselves. It gives them permission to talk to people that they otherwise wouldn't. It teaches them how to listen. It teaches them how to record and tell the smaller stories that will one day make up our history.

Sadly, journalism is still the ugly stepsister to English courses; when it is offered, it is often an elective course. Across the country, it is more and more common for districts to cut journalism courses and programs. It is time for English teachers to embrace journalism, to make sure that it is in every school. As an English teacher, I want my students to have the right to engage with members of our community and our world. I want them to call the White House, practice their speaking skills, and secure press passes for when the president comes to speak in our area. I want students to write sentences and to know that they are grammatically correct. I want students to know and understand the people and issues in our community. I want students to put faces on significant topics such as immigration. I want students to use words responsibly to capture life, to inform our communities, to inspire change, and to give hope. Students have the right to read and write, and journalism is the foundation of our democracy. If we don't start using our classrooms to foster student voices who use their First Amendment rights, then we are complacently participating in the quiet erosion of our democracy that starts within our classroom walls. As teachers, we have an important choice to make and an essential job to do.

Reflecting on Journalism Teaching and Students' Rights to Read and Write

Take some time to reflect on these questions, either by yourself or with colleagues.

1. How do you create classrooms where student responses are valued and an integral part of instruction? Have someone observe your teaching for a few class periods, and track when you are active as the teacher and when students are active. When students are active, are they creating new information or are they restating already known information?

2. How many response opportunities do students get during a class period? Are you the sole provider of response? Or do students get the opportunity to share their responses with peers?

3. How does student work extend outside of the classroom? How does it matter in the community and world that surrounds students?

4. What do students in your community care about? What issues are present in your community that students could research?

5. What are some easy ways that student work can be shared and have a place in the community? Social media? School publications? School meetings? Website?

It is up to us to let students know their rights and then to build our practice around supporting and protecting our students' rights to read and write.

References

Fleischer, C., & Andrew-Vaughan, S. (2009). *Writing outside your comfort zone: Helping students navigate unfamiliar genres.* Portsmouth, NH: Heinemann.

Tinker v. Des Moines Independent Community School District 393 US 503 (1969). *Student Press Law Center* (2000). Retrieved from http://www.splc.org/article/2000/12/tinker-v-des-moines-independent-community-school-district

Chapter Two

Linguistic Diversity: Strengthening Our Learning Communities

Cat Ragozzino

Linguistic diversity is an advantage for teachers and students involved in culturally diverse schools across the United States. Having students who are English Learners (ELs), bilingual students, multilingual students, and in some cases, students who speak a hybrid of colloquial home languages and have mastery of Basic Interpersonal Communicative Language Skills (BICS) but lack mastery in academic English language, is the reality of classroom compositions in many schools (Cummins, 1979). Recognizing this as our reality and being well informed about the language needs of students at varying levels of language acquisition can make our classrooms richer environments where the academic rigor and skills are never compromised, yet the scaffolding to bridge the language gap exists to support all learners. All students have a right to read and write and learn, regardless of their language backgrounds. Creating classroom environments in which ELs feel honored and respected, making grade-level academic content both accessible and rigorous for ELs, and welcoming students' cultural heritages as an integral part of our schools will allow these children to have equitable access to knowledge.

It is just as important to understand that we are *all* ELs, to varying degrees. Ask your US-born, native-English-speaking students where the *banister* is located in a house, or what a *mantle* is. Can they identify a *farce* from something stated *in earnest*? My point is that although the students with whom I work most closely—students who are labeled as ELs—are unique in that a linguistic *transfer* needs to occur from one language to another, *all* students are indeed learners of academic language. All children in every classroom are increasing their personal knowledge of academic English vocabulary as they engage with meaningful instruction—but that incremental growth halts the moment the instruction is not made accessible to them.

yes!

In my current urban district of Meriden, Connecticut, we have the good fortune to have four schools that house bilingual Spanish-English education programs. The percentage of ELs in Meriden as of June 2018 was 14.9, or 1,166 students. Of these students, 308 were enrolled in bilingual education, and 858 were enrolled in mainstream education and receiving ESOL services. Most of our ELs were from various Spanish-speaking countries, with varied, rich cultural heritage and backgrounds; we also had ELs who spoke other languages, including Arabic, Bangla, Bengali, Filipino, French, Italian, Pashto, Twi/Fante, Urdu, and Vietnamese, to name a handful. In the aftermath of Hurricane Irma and Hurricane Maria's Category 4 storms hitting Puerto Rico, we received children on a daily basis in our district, especially in schools housing bilingual education programs. At one of the middle schools where I work, I personally received more than a dozen post-hurricane survivors from Puerto Rico in my classes; district-wide, we received over 150. My students who were hurricane survivors were also coping with a great deal of trauma, which exacerbates their affective filter for potentially hindering language learning. One of my students watched both his *abuela* (grandmother) and his *tío* (uncle) die in the aftermath of the storm, in their family home as they suffered with no electricity, no road access to medical facilities, and limited food supplies. Another student had terrible scars up and down her arms, lacerations from shielding her head when her bedroom collapsed; a cousin in training to become a nurse had stitched her up the best she could. Others told me they couldn't sleep and had under-eye creases to show for it because their nightmares of the storm and its aftermath were too upsetting. In spite of such trauma, these children came to us eager to work, motivated to learn, and deeply appreciative of the safety of our schools and the stable infrastructure of this community. Events like this storm and the resulting influx of children who are ELs provide further proof that our teachers need to be trained in how to support ELs and support language acquisition for all students.

The right to read and write in the United States should be a universal standard. The fact is, however, that sometimes students whose parents are less vocal—whether it's because they culturally respect and look up to educational institutions and would never question the decisions made for their children, or because it's intimidating to address adults in a school when those parents do not fluently speak English—do not get placed into the most appropriately rigorous coursework tracks. This occurs, in my opinion, out of not knowing, or ignorance, about language acquisition by personnel who place students into classes. I have seen a child from South America, who had been in honors and advanced placement (AP) classes in her native country, placed into basic academic classes where students were far below grade level in reading ability. When I rushed to have the student put into AP and honors classes to correct this error, I was asked, "Why? She doesn't know how to speak English; she can't possibly keep up with the classwork in those classes." But what they didn't realize is that students who have the literacy skills in their L1, or native language, or understand concepts such as democracy or racism, or know what the scientific method is, will (with proper language support) experience a *transfer* of skills as they acquire their L2, or subsequent language. We cannot wait to teach them the content until they gain fluency in English. We must support the language growth as we teach the grade-level, adapted curricula.

Rights to an Accessible Education

What is most important to understand and something that I pass along to other educators is that all these students have a right to an accessible education, and it is our responsibility as educators to find a way to meet their needs. As an educator of children who are not native English speakers and who often have parents who feel as if they do not have a voice in the English-speaking school system, I am unapologetically an advocate for ELs with fellow teachers, department leaders, and administrators so that these children can receive the language supports they need to access grade-level, appropriate content, and also have access to meaningful educational activities. The 1974 *Lau v. Nichols* Supreme Court ruling states, "There is no equality of treatment merely by providing students with the same facilities, textbooks, teachers and curriculum for students who do not understand English [and therefore] are effectively foreclosed from meaningful education" (1974).

Having the knowledge, training, and tools to teach ELs is the best way to make academic content comprehensible to these students. I, along with two colleagues, have been training every new teacher who begins in the Meriden Public Schools with the Sheltered Instruction Observation Protocol (SIOP) method of teaching. The professional development is geared to give an abundance of examples of how to modify content lessons with language support while not compromising the academic rigor. Some tools include building background knowledge, providing sentence frames, working with manipulatives or realia, and using language-learning objectives for every lesson in which the goal is for students to be reading, writing, speaking, and listening to academic English. Our goal is to have teachers leave with a toolbox of how to modify their lessons to support ELs. More recently, we have continued that support to fellow educators in an ongoing coaching model so that the language support for our ELs in the district is consistently provided with great fidelity.

My students know that I jokingly refer to my classroom as "My House." In My House, my "kids" have meals, clean up, work hard, help their peers, give and get respect, and always have someone who cares for them. In Meriden, we have a federally grant-funded program so that every student is provided free breakfast and lunch. The learning environment is a joyful blend of food, friends, family, and academic accountability. I try to maintain a balance of rigorous academic work with high expectations, while also creating space and time for students to feel safe, valued, welcomed, and loved.

I begin the year setting a precedent that, every day, students are expected to state orally the date, the unit's content objectives, and the daily language objective. Our first unit is one where they must use sentence frames to ask questions in English, write the data and categorize the information in a graphic organizer, and eventually summarize their findings using certain academic vocabulary in written paragraphs with the support of modeling and sentence starters. Some students enter without knowing how to say, "My name is . . ." in English, while others have taken courses in English in their respective countries before moving to Connecticut. Those disparities do not change my classroom's objectives; rather, they determine how much scaffolding and support to provide. I encourage students to lean on one another to negotiate meaning and engage in translanguaging to use different languages and linguistic features to communicate and bridge understanding (Garcia, 2016).

Explicit instruction of academic vocabulary, providing language supports, and scaffolding lessons and activities with cognizance of how people learn language have been the foundations of my teaching methodology. But equally important is tapping into students' rich linguistic heritage, their beautiful cultural backgrounds, their familial support at home, and their overall self-efficacy and well-being. It is simply a humanistic right to be able to have a place and voice in an educational setting, and all of our students deserve that.

Families, in my experience, have frequently been under the false impression that they should immerse their children in English and therefore cease speaking in their home language outside of school. In our district, we sporadically take children into kindergarten whose families do not speak English at home, even though many of them were born in the United States. Sometimes these students come into kindergarten not knowing what colors or numbers are named *in any language*. I have learned, after speaking with the parents, that they were concerned that they would confuse their children if they taught them the colors and numbers in their native language; they wanted their children to succeed in the English-speaking schools, so they avoided talking with them about these things. This false impression unintentionally puts these children at a huge disadvantage when they enter school. Let me be clear: I have never come across a parent who did not care about their child or did not want to do what is best for them, but I have come across many who simply were not sure what to do. Communities, birth-to-three programs, public libraries, and other community organizations need to work more diligently to spread the message to parents of preschool-age children that learning the correct names for things in the home language, if that is the parent's strong and accurate tongue, can only help the linguistic transfer of knowledge occur when the children enter school! Understanding concepts—like the idea that a certain hue has a name, that different animals have different names, that pages in books are turned in one direction, and text is read left to right—regardless of what language these things are taught in, is paramount to setting children up for success in language and in school.

I have worked diligently to convey the message to parents that literacy skills transfer in most languages, and therefore they should continue to make an effort to speak—at length, and about rich and varied topics, rather than solely about the daily mundane mumblings and commands—so that their children develop strong linguistic skills in their first and subsequent languages. Placing value on this has the bonus perk of making students feel pride in their heritage; it lowers the affective filter for parents, and it welcomes a sense of belonging in my classroom where linguistic diversity is valued and celebrated (Krashen, 1981).

I taught secondary English (literature/language arts) for eight years to students whose first language was not English, and in the past five years I have taught English for Speakers of Other Languages (ESOL) to students in grades 6 through 8. The sheltered English classes, as they were called, allowed me to deliver the same grade-level skills and concepts while teaching some of the canonical texts that were expected to be taught to all high school students within the English curriculum. One aspect of the ESOL English classroom that is critical, however, to linguistic diversity and the process of language acquisition is the intentional and explicit attention to grammar, the use of cognates, and the frontloading of vocabulary. These intentional instructional practices help ELs bridge the language and build literacy skills.

Making Content Accessible to All Learners

Over the years, and with various texts, I have modified learning tasks, adapted texts, and scaffolded learning activities to make content comprehensible to ELs in my

English literature classes, but I will go into detail on what I did with one particular unit. The invention of and current ease of access to resources like computers, online videos and images, and online translation programs have made much of the labor that used to be involved in this process a lot easier for teachers, which is an undeniable benefit for our students. Any time that I could incorporate or bridge students' culture with the teaching of classical literature, the more permeating the lesson or theme would be for my students. Bridging culture is a key component of allowing students who are ELs to have an equal access to reading and writing in classrooms.

One year, it was an expectation that all students in the eleventh grade read *The Great Gatsby* (Fitzgerald, 1925). At the time, I had two classes composed of all newcomer students (having arrived in the United States in the last three years, and all at the beginning levels of English language acquisition) who spoke various languages. Each class size was around twenty, and in both classes I had a handful of native Spanish speakers, some French speakers, some Mandarin speakers, a few Bengali speakers, and then a handful of students who each spoke a different language and didn't have peers of their same language background. For the purpose of this chapter, I will focus on the efforts made to meet the needs of my Spanish-speaking students, but it should be noted that modifications such as translations of key vocabulary, images, sentence frames, and other supports were put in place for all students, regardless of their native language. The task of reading F. Scott Fitzgerald's sophisticated novel was understandably an arduous one. This occurred before the 2013 film *The Great Gatsby* had been created and was quite a few years before teachers had any computer projectors in their classrooms, so no YouTube, no Google Images, no student electronic devices of any kind. Nearly every support I used I created by drawing it myself, using transparencies over photocopies of the text on my overhead projector, or creating interaction strategies where students read parts of the text from notecards on which I had pasted photocopied passages of text. If I were teaching this now, I would certainly have built background knowledge by using selected clips of the film, short videos to show American culture during that era, or Google Images to provide visuals for key vocabulary, and when necessary, by allowing students to use Google Translate to understand key vocabulary or concepts.

I began by determining the grade-level expectations for the skills all eleventh graders were supposed to master through reading *The Great Gatsby*. These included analyzing character development, improving reading comprehension, and gaining an understanding of the parts of a dramatic novel. From there, it was imperative to select important chapters and specific scenes from the novel that would showcase these components and allow students to practice the expected literacy skills.

The scene at the beginning of the novel, when Daisy Buchanan, Jordan Baker, Tom Buchanan, and Nick Carraway are talking, is an important one to begin studying character development and analyzing the different personalities. For this scene, I extracted the words spoken by each character and wrote the scene as if it were a play. Students were assigned roles and had to act out their characters after some pantomiming help from me, to set the stage for their personalities. For example, Daisy is a very spoiled character who complains dramatically about how hot the weather is. To represent her, I would drape myself over a classroom chair and speak her lines with the intonation indicated by Fitzgerald's writing. Students who did not feel comfortable reading aloud in front of the room worked quietly at stations on the blackboard, writing down characteristics from a list I had provided them ahead of time, while negotiating meaning with one other to describe each character based on the performed scene. By the end of class, all students were able to write an initial analysis of the four characters, stating which characters were aggressive, fragile, competitive, and so on.

Another task that worked well with this particular novel and tied into students' interests was through the love many had of telenovelas. (There was a popular one at that time, and its dramatic and tumultuous plot twists and turns rivaled the histrionics of *Gatsby* fairly well.) Using this tactic did not leave behind students from other countries and cultures, for soap operas reflect the dramatic family and romantic interactions that are a part of *human nature*, not just of one group of people. For teaching this novel, presenting portions of the book to the students as a telenovela lent itself well to the love affair of Daisy and Tom Buchanan, and the gruesome and melodramatic demise of Myrtle Wilson. For this, I first tape-recorded the theme song of a popular telenovela at the time from Telemundo. Then I took a scene from the book in which readers learned of Tom Buchanan's affair, but rewrote the text in shorter sentences that were more manageable for my English Learners, and used cognates any time they were available. For example, if I wanted to convey a description of Tom Buchanan, I would take a quotation like "two shining, arrogant eyes had established dominance over his face, and gave him the appearance of always leaning aggressively forward . . . you could see a great pack of muscle shifting when his shoulder moved under his thin coat" (Fitzgerald, 1925, p. 5) and both shorten the sentence and include the Spanish-English cognates, so it would read as "Tom was an arrogant and dominant man. He was aggressive and muscular." This worked well for the Spanish speakers in the class because *arrogante* is a cognate for *arrogant*, *dominante* is a cognate for *dominant*, *agresivo* is a cognate for *aggressive*, and *muscular* is spelled exactly the same way in both English and Spanish. Although I have spoken at length about modifying learning tasks for a class comprising mostly Spanish speakers, because that was the composition of my classes at the time, these scaffolds can be adapted to multiple-language classrooms.

Indeed, inviting any and all components of students' native cultures and interests into the classroom is an excellent way to bridge the learning and increase student motivation when the language barrier is such a difficult hurdle for students to overcome.

I used the same approach to summarize a handful of dramatic scenes—such as the reunion of Gatsby and Daisy, the fight between Tom and Gatsby, and the car accident—and had students read the scenes aloud and act them out, or read in small groups and then fill out graphic organizers to show how characters' actions revealed their motivations and personalities. Graphic organizers might be arranged to show how the actions or words of one character incited reactive behavior from another character, or show how one event in the story led to another event in a chain reaction, to help students analyze the relationships between characters and events. By the end of the novel, some of my more intermediate and advanced students would take passages from the text that I had extracted for them and summarize on their own in this same manner.

Scaffolding for Varying Student Needs

I have great respect for the original language of classical literature, so I am always cognizant of exposing students to that language over the course of a unit of study in a supported manner, without modifying or adapting the text. And nearly equally important, I have a sensitivity to teenagers' emotional need to fit in and not feel singled out by having a different text from their peers. One way I would do this for my ELs at varying language abilities was to select a passage or page ahead of time that I wanted students to read and analyze, and highlight or underline parts of the text using overhead transparencies with photo corners. To differentiate this literary analysis activity for various student needs, I would simply provide the quotation on which we were focusing on the board and give the page number to students who were capable in the higher intermediate and advanced stages of language development; for students who required more language support, I would use a clear sheet of plastic to highlight or underline that quotation, and include translations of key vocabulary or even drawings if the passage called for it to ensure understanding. Ahead of time, I would fit the transparency to the book page and stick photo corners to the outer corner; then, sliding it onto the selected page, I would use Expo markers to make notes and highlight the key parts of the text. This way, every student received the physical high school–distributed novel, and no one's looked different from the outside, but my students who needed help to extract meaning from the language on the page had the support sneakily provided. At the beginning of the year, I would individually hand out these books with or without the transparency supports to the students based on their language needs; later on in the year, as students' trust increased and they became accustomed to my language-learning classroom, I'd simply make a stack of them available next to the textbooks or novels and allow students to use them at their own discretion.

The Adventures of Huckleberry Finn (Twain, 1994) was another class text used later in the year. Students had the choice between three stacks of differing versions: some textbooks; some textbooks loaded with sticky notes and transparency overlays; and some photocopied packets with key passages highlighted, as well as annotations and key vocabulary explained in the margins. One question I get sometimes is whether all the students opt to use the version with the most support, whether they need it or not—and the answer is that in twelve years of teaching, I have never seen that yet. I am always impressed by students who push themselves when they are met with a teacher who challenges them while also providing support so that success is attainable.

Reflecting on Linguistic Diversity and Students' Rights to Read and Write

Take some time to reflect on these questions, either by yourself or with colleagues.

1. Think about a lesson or unit that you regularly teach. What skills are you aiming for your students to master? What language constructs or vocabulary do they need in English to access these skills?

2. What might be potential barriers for students that will prevent them from engaging in a way that will help them progress toward college and career readiness? What actions could be taken in the classroom during instruction to remove one of those barriers?

3. How can you use students' cultural backgrounds, heritage, familial relationships, and experiences to strengthen this lesson, experience, or classroom?

4. How can you plan your lessons to support the learning of academic language for all students?

5. How else might you support English Learners' rights to read and write?

The Loud Language-Learning Classroom

My classroom and most language-learning classrooms are loud. But not with side conversations and off-topic banter; rather, with the ongoing chatter of students who are allowed to negotiate meaning with each other throughout a lesson. The negotiation of meaning is very simply having students check with one another in a language in which they are most comfortable for the accuracy of their understanding of the content. For example, in discussing *Wonder* (Palacio, 2012), students ask, "What's she talking about?" and "When it describes Auggie, what is wrong with his face?" It takes time and good classroom management to establish this classroom environment where students are able to chat with one another to make sure they are understanding the activity, task, or content accurately; but once they know the classroom is a safe place to use their language to bridge the gap between their native knowledge and the new information being given, this expedites and enhances their language learning. What takes *more* time, for me, is becoming accustomed to the noise level of a classroom where this is allowed! But in a classroom with linguistic diversity and students who are all going through the similar struggles of language learning, offering a place where they may use their first language with each other while also being supported in using English lowers that affective filter that Krashen (1981) says can hinder language learning.

Conclusion

It is a gift and my humble opportunity to be a part of my students' lives as they charge through the emotionally and cognitively challenging process of learning English. What my students bring to my classroom, with their rich and varied cultural backgrounds, experiences, and knowledge, enriches and enhances any textbook lesson that I could ever offer. Welcoming linguistic diversity in our classrooms and maintaining academic rigor while giving students their legal right to meaningful language supports and activities will strengthen our classrooms, our schools, and our communities.

References

Cummins, J. (1979). Cognitive/academic language proficiency, linguistic interdependence, the optimum age question and some other matters. *Working Papers on Bilingualism, 19*(121–29).

Fitzgerald, F. S. (1925). *The Great Gatsby*. New York, NY: Charles Scribner's Sons.

Garcia, O., Johnson, S. I., & Selzer, K. (2016). *The Translanguaging classroom: Leveraging student bilingualism for learning*. Philadelphia, PA: Caslon.

Krashen, S. (1981). *Second language acquisition and second language learning*. Oxford, United Kingdom: Pergamo.

Lau v. Nichols, 414 U.S. 563 (1974). Retrieved from https://en.wikipedia.org/wiki/Lau_v._Nichols

Palacio, R. J. (2012). *Wonder*. New York, NY: Alfred A. Knopf.

Twain, M. (1994). *The Adventures of Huckleberry Finn*. London, United Kingdom: Penguin Books.

Chapter Three

Danger of Perpetuating Stereotypes: Muslim Students' Rights to Literacy in the English Classroom

Elma Rahman

Because we live in an age when media dictates the way society perceives groups of people, specifically those who are minorities or who have been marginalized, we must all be aware of both the stereotypes that are perpetuated by media and how these stereotypes may affect the lives of those belonging to minoritized groups. Having been a Muslim American student in the US public school system and now an ELA teacher in New York City, I have seen and felt the backlash of such perpetuation in action. This stereotyping and the ease with which it is accepted made me realize that children lose something special at a very early age: the will and ability to read about all groups of people and to express one's views and thoughts in harmony with others, regardless of and perhaps with respect to our differences. This loss directly contradicts the belief of NCTE that "the expression of ideas without fear of censorship is a fundamental right" (NCTE, 2014, p. xxi). Specifically, I fear how we as a society will be able to combat the constant misrepresentation, as images of Muslims in media lead to Muslim students either self-censoring or complying with what is considered the norm. People, and especially teachers, must find ways to help others develop a stance of empathy and understanding toward those who are different from themselves. If we take the bond that exists between students and teachers and use that to cultivate a mindset that is accepting of differences and respectful of multiple perspectives, we may be able to dispel a fear of judgment so that students can come out of their shells and engage in meaningful class discussions that will impact the lives of every individual present in that classroom, regardless of or with respect for their various identities. To guide students along this process of open-ended and meaningful learning, teachers can model for students by sharing the multiplicity of their own identities.

In *Teaching for Diversity and Social Justice*, Adams, Bell, Goodman, and Joshi define social justice education as "an interdisciplinary conceptual framework for analyzing multiple forms of oppression and their intersections, as well as a set of interactive, experiential pedagogical principles and methods/practices" (2016, p. 4). In relation to the ELA classroom, the key terms here are "multiple forms of oppression and their interactions," for as students and teachers, we can examine many examples of oppression, in literature and in history, that people from various minority groups have endured. As a teacher, committed to upholding students' rights to read and write, I began to wonder what I could do to help students avoid perpetuating negative stereotypes about Muslims—especially since such stereotypes impact both Muslims and non-Muslims. Both groups may self-censor, out of fear of either being associated with the stereotype or being labeled as racist.

Through the course of this chapter, then, I relate three ways of teaching for social justice in three different teaching contexts that invite a foregrounding of Muslim identities.

1. The first context is a workshop with educators, college professors, and aspiring teachers. Here, I consider teaching for social justice with respect to religion in general but Islam in particular by challenging teachers and students to get out of their comfort zones through the tenets of *autoethnography*.

2. The second context is a focus group discussion among Roman Catholic girls about religion and interfaith friendship. Here, I consider teaching for social justice with attention to Islam by engaging in *critical literacy*.

3. The third context is my ninth-grade ELA classroom in a private Islamic school in Queens. Here, I consider teaching for social justice with respect to Muslim Americans by creating contexts for *vicarious learning*.

Across these ways of teaching and across these teaching contexts, I advocate on behalf of students' rights to read and write.

Autoethnography

Before I discuss the workshop, I will briefly reflect on an experience I had while student teaching. I was in a ninth-grade classroom, and I remember a student randomly mentioning 9/11 and terrorist attacks. During that period, my cooperating teacher was instructing the lesson, and I was grading papers in the back of the class. Although I knew that part of the reason the teacher did not address the question and rather asked the student to pay attention to the lesson at hand was so the lesson would not go off topic, I was keenly aware that she, like most teachers, wanted to avoid that particular subject altogether on the basis of how uncomfortable the discussion could become for both the Muslim and non-Muslim students in the class. I also remember being relieved that it was not me instructing the class that day because I would not have known how to facilitate such a discussion. In retrospect, though, I realize that it could have been a teachable moment had the right classroom rules and environment been established. If circumstances had been different, perhaps I could have shared with the class a different perspective on terrorists and how terrorist does not equate to Muslim, or given some of the Muslim students in the class an opportunity to clarify any misconceptions. For example, if I had taken that moment to hit pause on my planned lesson and engaged the class in a word study on the word *terror* and then discussed the goals of people throughout history as well as in the present who hope to incite fear in others, the class could have arrived at a more holistic understanding of the word. We could then have discussed the ramifications of labeling a whole group based on the actions of some in the group, and elaborated the point through examples of similar occurrences that students see in their own lives.

It was a year later when I conducted a workshop with a cluster of college students, student teachers, and faculty at Queens College in a series called Complicated Conversations. My segment was titled "Breaking the Mold: The Teacher as an Individual," and in it I presented some of my research on the importance of a teacher's individual identity and also led a discussion on the perception of Muslims in today's society (Caraballo & Rahman, 2016). As one of the activities of the workshop, the attendees read excerpts from Nathaniel Hawthorne's short story "The Minister's Black Veil," set in Puritan New England, about a young minister named Mr. Hooper. One day, before delivering his sermon, Mr. Hooper decides that he will wear a black veil over his face until the end of his days, which causes the Puritans of the community to fear the veil and what it represents. The task I invited participants to try was to analyze the symbolism of the veil and compare its meaning and representation to that of the *niqab*, the black veil worn by many Muslim women, including myself. During this experience, what struck me most was the fact that even adults can be found to self-censor out of fear of being judged or labeled.

In a whole-group discussion, I asked people to volunteer to share their thoughts on the *niqab*. I knew that I was asking some of them to step out of their comfort zones by posing such a question when I was standing in front of them wearing a *niqab* myself. A few individuals responded with complete ease, sharing that they were not bothered by it in any way since we all live in Queens, which is a very diverse area. One woman said that even though it did not matter to her if a Muslim woman wore a veil, she could understand why some people may feel wary. Encouraged by her response, others joined in, careful not to cause any hurt feelings but admitting that sometimes they felt unsure about it because it made them nervous not to be able to see someone's face. I told them that even though I am a Muslim woman who wears the face veil, I believe that this is a legitimate concern. Would it, I asked them, ease people's minds if they were able to have open discussions that can enlighten everyone present about why such worries are understandable as well as why Muslim women also have a right to cover their faces if they wish?

When I then asked the group to complete a Venn diagram as they compared a picture of me wearing a *niqab* and an image of Hawthorne's Mr. Hooper, they were much more willing to share their thoughts, perhaps for two reasons: first, it was not as personal since it was not a live person they were analyzing but an image; and second, they were able to work in small groups to determine various reasons people may have to cover their faces. With regard to the similarities they found between Mr. Hooper and my selfie, they stated that both veils were black, meant to cover the faces of their bearers. In terms of difference, they noticed that the minister in the story wore the veil to consciously instill fear among the people of the town, unlike the purpose for wearing the *niqab*, which is to cover a woman's identity and beauty from the gazes of strangers. These students, student teachers, and faculty came to the realization on their own that since the eras are different, the purposes are also not the same. The person in the selfie is simply showing people in her own way that she is Muslim and this is how she practices her faith. At the end of the task and discussion, I suggested to these educators and future teachers that completing an activity such as this exemplified how when we are in our own classrooms, with the right questions and strategies, we can open the doors to discussions that are otherwise difficult to address, and we can help clear up misunderstandings and stereotypes perpetuated by the media.

In the final part of the workshop, I shared the work that I accomplished with Sharon Jackson when I taught her novella, *Fajr*, in my high school classroom. *Fajr* is a story about the conflicts between Muslim and Jewish communities and the hope that grows from interfaith friendship. The story is about a Muslim teenage girl named Fajr who was pushed to her death by two Jewish men. When her cousin Haithm, in his grief over her loss, decides to retaliate against the Jewish community, Fajr's ghost turns to her Jewish counterpart, an Orthodox boy named Adam, who is the only one who can see her. Although initially mistrusting of each other, the two form a unique friendship as they work toward saving Haithm from making a mistake and becoming someone he hates, a person who for personal motives gives Islam a bad name. The reason to use this story as a parting note for the workshop was to turn the discussion toward redesigning curriculum so that it would be inclusive of all groups of people, and could address controversial topics and conflicts students may not otherwise be exposed to in a safe and academic setting. By doing so, we promote not only multicultural education but social justice education as well, in which students acquire awareness and respect for different cultures, races, and religions.

By opening myself up to my audience and positioning myself in relation to how I may be perceived in society, I began engaging in autoethnographic practices that propelled others to share their thoughts as well. This approach of focusing on oneself as a starting point for critical analysis of the topics and issues we encounter in the ELA classroom stems from my personal experience and the fact that as a student, things seemed interesting and important to me once I was able to relate them to my life or hypothetically put myself in a situation that I was not likely to encounter. Similarly, I learned that only after we voice our thoughts on the issues and injustices in our lives do we become perceptive about them in the lives of others. Not only does taking this approach help us to empathize with others, but it also encourages us to think as problem solvers rather than just brushing off the issue, a core goal of social justice education. This process of self-reflection in order to connect what is personal with what is cultural or societal is called autoethnography, which I believe is essential in order for students to engage in critical literacy (Duarte, 2007).

From Autoethnography to Critical Literacy

In his article "What Is Critical Literacy?," Ira Shor (1999) writes that critical literacy, an approach to education that requires close examination of texts to find underlying meanings, "challenges the status quo in an effort to discover alternative paths for self and social development" (p. 1). Throughout my journey to become an educator, I constantly found myself engaging in critical literacy—first as a college student discussing major issues in education with my professors and peers, then as a student teacher trying to prove to myself and others that there is a place for Muslim women in the public school system, and finally, as a teacher assisting my students in asking questions about social norms and who dictates them. Taking such an approach in my own teaching and classroom allowed my students and me to connect with each other and with the texts we were reading in class in a way that opened doors to question why things are the way they are, and whether there are things in our lives that need further exploration in order to bring about change that will benefit us all.

When I first asked my students to think critically—a goal of all literacy teachers—and urged them to consider why a certain author may have a particular viewpoint on any given topic, I was met with either blank or confused stares. On the one hand, I wanted them to analyze the topic objectively to make a judgment for themselves, but on the other hand, I wanted them to understand that authors do have particular perspectives and also to question what lies behind those perspectives. Their stares asked me, "What does that even mean?" In that moment, I realized that I owed it to my class to explain what I meant by perspective, how perspective connects to critical literacy, and what it would mean to move beyond the approaches to critical thinking they had been asked to engage in until now. The approach to critical thinking they would practice in our class, they came to understand, included how they should tackle conflicts, ask questions, and find solutions—the essence of critical literacy. I wanted them to begin by asking a simple question whenever we encountered a new topic, issue, or idea: Why should this matter to me?

In order to examine how different groups of students perceive interfaith friendship in a time of social and global crisis, I worked with the author of *Fajr* to read the text with a focus group that summer. My experience during the summer course was in many ways very different from working with my own ELA class in the Islamic school during my first year of teaching. First, these students did not know me until it came time to read the story during a class meeting over the summer. Also, instead of having them read the novella on their own for homework, Sharon and I read the story aloud with the focus group with pauses for questions and discussion. To help students take an autoethnographic approach to relate with the text, I modeled for them by openly reflecting on what it was like for me to be a Muslim girl in New York City and how that relates to Fajr's experiences. I told them about the first time I was called a terrorist because I was wearing a *hijab* (Islamic headcover); I did not even know what it meant since I was only twelve years old, just a few months after the 9/11 attack. This seemed to resonate with one student because her best friend was a Muslim girl. I also disclosed how sometimes, when I would see a Jewish person or family on the street, I would behave awkwardly because I did not know exactly how to react. From here, Sharon and I took the conversation in a direction that allowed students to express whether they were able to relate to any of the characters in the narrative. One student shared that while she understood why Haithm was so angry and upset, his reasons did not justify his idea of setting a *yeshiva*, a Jewish school, on fire, because it would be wrong to hurt a community for the mistake of two individuals. The students then discussed the novella in relation to their own perception of Muslims and Jews because faith and religion were major themes in the novel, and these students were all Roman Catholic. They analyzed the conflicts between the people belonging to the two faiths, how such issues impacted the youth of these communities, and how friendship could potentially open doors for reconciliation, if not on a grand or global level, then perhaps on a local or societal level.

When I asked them to share whether the story related to them in a personal way, as it did for me, one student responded that she was not even aware that the tension between Muslims and Jews could be so intense in the United States. When I asked my lead-in question for critical literacy, "Why should it matter to me?," I realized that the tenth graders' reception was different from the way my previous group of Muslim students had responded. For example, perhaps as outsiders to the two faiths in the story, they were readily able to accept interfaith friendship, one girl sharing that her best friend was Muslim. Also, their attention shifted to the injustices that are faced by both individuals and societies as one of them shared some of the prejudices she experienced because she is Latina and how those relate to some of the characters' experiences in the narrative. Another significant element of my work with the focus group is that even though we did not explicitly discuss stereotypes and the ways that they are perpetuated, the takeaway for these students was a newfound awareness of injustice because of past history and present media as they admitted that much of what they knew about both Muslims and Jews came from what they saw and heard through media.

Vicarious Learning

In my own ninth-grade ELA class consisting of twelve Muslim students—two boys and ten girls—in a private Islamic school, I combined critical literacy techniques and the tenets of autoethnography with the facilitation of vicarious learning in the classroom. According to behaviorist and psychologist Albert Bandura (1971), vicarious learning is a social-cognitive theory proposing that students learn by observing one another, especially when they realize that the other student is a recipient of some kind of reinforcement or reward. It goes hand in hand with Lev Vygotsky's social constructivism, a theory that both emphasizes the social contexts in which learning takes place and demonstrates how students develop skills by building on what they already know (Powell & Kalina, 2009). Students, this theory suggests, learn best when they learn from us as well as from one another. Applying a combination of these two approaches to implement social justice education at a time when Muslim students as well as the Muslim community are often oppressed through misrepresentation in media and misconceptions in society helps all students learn collaboratively and be intuitive and empathetic toward one another's identities and the injustices they may face for their differences.

When my ninth-grade students read *Fajr*, instantly they were able to make connections to their own identities and experiences as Muslims; they also shared their questions, concerns, and preconceptions about practicing Jews. For these students, reading a narrative such as *Fajr* proved to be a novel experience because it was the first time they had encountered a protagonist such as Fajr, who deals with many of the stereotypes regarding Muslims that these students face every day. An autoethnographic approach to discussing certain elements of the novella came as second nature for these students because the conflicts within the novella were so relevant to their lives, such as having an awkward encounter with someone wearing a *yarmulke*, a cap worn by many Orthodox Jewish men, or having to wear a *hijab* in the streets of New York City, where some people will smile at you and be kind while others will make derogatory comments. These events in the narrative resonated with my students because they then related incidents that were similar from their own experiences. In hindsight, I know that the conversations would have been much different had all the students not shared the same faith. Almost all of the students were either sharing similar anecdotes or agreeing with one another's viewpoints.

To encourage students to work constructively together and think about the different sides of the story, I asked them to consider some of the conflicts that members of the Jewish community may face, because the coprotagonist of the narrative is a Jewish boy named Adam. At first, the students struggled with this question. To jump-start the discussion, I invited students to list some of the negative stereotypes associated with Muslims; and they were able to compose quite a long list. I then asked them to do the same for Jews. The students themselves pointed out that this particular list was not as long. When I inquired why that may be, one student replied that perhaps it was because they did not know much about Jews, and whatever they did know came from their parents or older relatives. To avoid perpetuating a negative view of any religion or identity marker and simultaneously demonstrate how these stereotypes are spread, I highlighted the irony that this is an issue Muslims face every day, that most people do not get the opportunity to know the true nature of Islam because they learn all the negative stereotypes from media and the prejudices of their elders. Vicariously, since it led to the need for validation of a different perspective, this conversation propelled another student to state that part of the reason some of their parents may be wary of Jews is because of the conflicts in the Middle East. Another student, clarifying that she was playing devil's advocate, said that based on that, it would be okay for people to mistrust Muslims since the 9/11 attack was conducted by people sharing the same faith as us. At this point in the conversation, I expressed to my class how exciting the discussion was, because it demonstrated that this was an issue that would be beneficial to talk about in class, and that the story itself could lead us to some solutions.

The takeaway for my ninth graders after reading and discussing *Fajr* was a newfound understanding of the Jewish community and an idea of the hope of overcoming the misconceptions one group of people may have about another.

Reflecting on Teaching Muslim Students and Students' Rights to Read and Write

Take some time to reflect on these questions, either by yourself or with colleagues.

1. How do you identify which students are marginalized in school and society?

2. Do you notice students self-censoring when sharing their thoughts and ideas in class discussion?

3. What do you see as the differences between incorporating critical literacy with critical thinking as opposed to just pushing students to become critical thinkers? What is the impact of these approaches on the students you teach?

4. Do you ever avoid topics regarding race, religion, and sexuality in order to keep classroom conversation "safe"?

5. What would be the benefits and challenges of modifying the current curriculum in order to include topics such as religion and belief systems in which complicated ideas are brought to light?

6. How often do you share your own thoughts and experiences with the class in order to encourage students to find their own voices?

Conclusion

When talk and discussion of religion enter the classroom, a fear of dogmatism and indoctrination arises for many people, from parents and school administrators to educators and even students. Many believe that if religion is to be discussed, it should be done with objectivity. NCTE believes that it is never the job of a teacher to indoctrinate students. Indeed, indoctrination should never be in the agenda of any educator. Instead, our job is to provide our students with multiple perspectives and help them analyze why people have certain views so that students can formulate their own beliefs and ideas while respecting or at least understanding those that are different from their own. If students begin to trust their school environment enough to share their beliefs, religious or other, then who are we as educators to stop or sway the discussion toward neutral and safe directions? Having been a Muslim student in the New York City public school system and now as a teacher, I am conscious of every time I feared that what I would say or write might be received with derision or judgment. As a teacher, it became even clearer to me that it is not only the Muslim students who suffer this way, but all students. Reading texts about the experiences of all people, sharing our autoethnographies, and encouraging students to do the same while simultaneously asking the critical question "Why should this matter to me?" is how I believe educators can help their students think about bringing change to society so that we can expel one misconception, one stereotype, and one injustice at a time.

References

Adams, M., Bell, L. A., Goodman, D. J., & Joshi, K. Y. (2016). *Teaching for diversity and social justice*. New York, NY: Routledge.

Bandura, A. (1971). Vicarious and self-reinforcement processes. In R. Glaser (Ed.), *The nature of reinforcement: A symposium of the Learning Research and Development Center, University of Pittsburgh* (pp. 228–78). New York, NY: Academic Press.

Caraballo, L., & Rahman, E. (2016). Visible teaching, (in)visible teacher: An educator's journey as a Muslim woman. *English Journal, 106*(2), 47–53.

Duarte, F. P. (2007). Using autoethnography in the scholarship of teaching and learning: Reflective practices from "the other side of the mirror." *International Journal for the Scholarship of Teaching and Learning, 1*(2), 1–11.

Hawthorne, N. (1832). The minister's black veil (J. Lynch, Ed.). (Original source *Mosses from an Old Manse*, vol. 1. New York, NY: Wiley & Putnam, 1846.) Retrieved from http://andromeda.rutgers.edu/~jlynch/Texts/ministersblackveil.html

National Council of Teachers of English (NCTE). (2014, July 31). *NCTE beliefs about the students' right to write [SRW]* [Position Statement]. Retrieved from http://www2.ncte.org/statement/students-right-to-write/

Powell, K. C., & Kalina, C. J. (2009). Cognitive and social constructivism: Developing tools for an effective classroom. *Education, 130*(2), 241–49. Academic OneFile. Retrieved from http://go.galegroup.com.queens.ezproxy.cuny.edu:2048/ps/i.do?p=AONE&sw=w&u=cuny_queens&v=2.1&it=r&id=GALE%7CA216181184&asid=6839c765d1d001175f43385b4ffc995c

Shor, I. (1999). What is critical literacy? *Journal for Pedagogy, Pluralism & Practice, 4*(1), 1–26. Retrieved from http://mediaeducation.org.mt/wp-content/uploads/2013/05/What-is-Critical-Literacy.pdf

Black Lives Matter: Disrupting Oppression by Identifying Hidden Narratives in the English Language Arts Classroom

Arianna Talebian

June 2016: A Classroom Conversation

A sea of confused Black and Brown faces set in

Engraved themselves into my point of vision

As I had to hold my hand to chest to get the next word out—

As twenty-four sets of eyes looked up to a 94 degree angle,

For an answer.

There are levels to this pain,

There are deep engrained roots of the history code encrypted on
    your school transcript,

That proposed you in this conversation,

That you are now engaged in this conversation.

Married to the fight of *All Lives* versus *Black Lives* that lead this
    conversation.

Turned desks to face your peer when you hear their story

That mirrors your story

The one that defines your race—humanity.

Questions begin to flood our walls,
As you begin to stand one by one to take turns writing your scripts on
the paper.
Weighing down with thoughts,
Questions,
Heavy with questions,
As we talk through this, we have to talk through this; we *have to* get
through this.

-*Ok, I understand #AllLivesMatter isn't saying Black lives don't matter*
    -*Why did they have to change it into All Lives, why can't it be Black lives?*
-*#AllLives includes Black lives*
-*Yea . . . But . . . Black lives have been suffering and oppressed for so long, I
don't think it's fair to push it all into one category.*
-*But we're all the same, we are all humans, we all matter*
    -*Were the officers thinking that when they shot . . .*
    -*Murdered!*
    -*My fault, murdered, those Black and Brown bodies?*
-*No. You're right, but they abused their power. Not all cops are the same, we
can't push it all into one. Remember*
-*Yea but they push Muslims into one too. Like that dude who shot up the bar
in Orlando. Or even since 9/11, we say that all Muslims are terrorists and
they are not.*
-*It was a bar that happened to have majority gay men and Latino men in
there*
-*Yea, #BlackLivesMatter isn't inclusive of them . . . wouldn't #AllLives be?*
-*No one is saying they shouldn't be included. We're saying right now, Black
and Brown lives matter the most. Why can't they have the attention?*
-*They do—They can*
-*The #AllLives Matter movement is selfish. It's not fair. You don't find it odd
that in 2012, when strong Black women created this movement as a call to
action after 17-year-old Trayvon Martin was posthumously placed on trial for
his own murder and the killer, George Zimmerman, was not held accountable
for the crime he committed. It was a response to the anti-Black racism that
permeates our society and also, unfortunately, our movement . . .*
    -*YAS girl.*
-*That shortly after, this 'movement' came about to be. Did they feel slighted?
Did they feel the need to exist? As if they didn't exist . . .*
-*When you say 'they' do you mean white people?*
    -*Yes*

-But #AllLives is talking about Latinos too.

  -Latinos are Black

-We are all the same

-We are not all treated the same. Blacks have been segregated for so many years—in schools, churches, and water fountains for crying out loud

-water.

-Can we real quick talk about how we're living in a time of the New Jim Crow? How, what was that statistic that we read from Just Mercy? *One in every three Black and Brown males born after the year 2001 will spend some time in jail or prison? How we still can't even vote, how we get labels attached to us, how we're enslaved even in a time where slavery doesn't 'exist' or does it? It does, it does. Forget water—we're not even drinking. Man, we're not even living. We are waking up in fear, walking in fear, I got my mother praying I don't become a hash tag before I become a leader in my community, I got my guard up when people wanna take pictures of me and my girl at a party because when I die are they going to use the one of me with a red solo cup in my hand? Or they gonna use the one of me, god willing, walking across the stage during graduation. Or the one of me feeding my baby sister, the one that I have to rush to pick up after school so I couldn't join the debate team but I debated in my heart. I'm sorry.*

  -Why are you apologizing bro?

  -Because they've conditioned us to apologize. For everything.

-You shouldn't be sorry

  -Should you? For using that hash tag?

-I don't use it, I just understand it.

  -I, I . . . understand it too

-We need to begin to understand each other. You see how we all fight about petty nonsense in the hallways; we need to unite before they take us all down.

-Well we cannot lose hope, that's what they want us to do.

  -So where does it start? When does it start?

It starts here.

Here, where—

Alton Sterling and Philando Castile wrote my curriculum.

Sleepless nights that lead into healing mornings, anxious and confused, stronger and more aware—

Here, where this circle was set up in such a way we can look in each
other's eyes
Where we can learn to constructively argue,
Disruptively disrupt societal oppressions
Selectively choose our words that can endorse, change, and heal other
Reluctantly release the earmuffs we wear during a conversation about
race, let out the warmth, to hear the truth.
Proactively come to conclusions, strategies, devices that can help
us continue down a path of healing, understanding and ultimately
transforming

*-Everyone is saying Black Lives Matter but in all reality, every life no matter
your skin color. I believe that Black lives aren't the only ones that matter right
now all over the world there's people's lives being taken away that we don't
even know about so it shouldn't only be Black people's lives that matter but
everyone else's too.*
-The #AllLives Matter movement cannot exist without #BlackLivesMatter
-People of color face the brunt of police brutality because they're minorities
*-Cops should be punished for placing false accusation on people who didn't do
anything*
    -All lives cannot matter until Black and Brown ones do.

Alton Sterling and Philando Castile wrote my curriculum.

I spent the majority of my junior year in the high school auditorium escaping
into the magnificent world of literature. I could not connect with my immediate
environment; my peers had no sense of my struggle. I remember reading *As I Lay
Dying* (Faulkner, 1930/1991) and thinking that if the story of burying one's mother
could be spoken about through fifteen different narrations, then surely there had to
be a way for me, a youth of color, to narrate my life. My narration, though different from the ones told by my peers, would eventually lead me to the place where I
wanted to be. The works of Faulkner resonated but didn't respond. What I learned
from my high school experience was that the canon of literature needed to be de-
constructed. My cries were silent, no sound or expression was made, but with each
passing day they became louder in my mind. The sounds were those of oppressed
bodies, the ones who weren't acknowledged in the walls of my classrooms, the ones
I knew I wanted to make the voice of my classroom when I became a teacher.

[handwritten margin note: How many of our students feel this way?]

As a teacher, I know that my understanding of the classroom is not narrated through me. It is, similar to Faulkner's fifteen voices, told through my hundreds of students. It changes steadily throughout time as things and people—including students—evolve. It changes compellingly through them, as they grow, mature, and find themselves. However, most important, it tweaks itself every time movements such as Black Lives Matter (BLM) spark. The writing and critical analysis of young people must serve as possibilities for reframing the narrative. An ELA classroom must not only deconstruct literature but also foster unique styles of writing as tools used to promote equity and engage trauma, as we prepare ourselves and our students to participate productively in movements aimed at achieving justice directly within our community. Furthermore, we must contextualize linguistic and cultural identities grounded in a broader national discussion on race and the movement of #BlackLivesMatter. #BlackLivesMatter is more than a movement; it is the reality in which young people are confronted regularly.

As the NCTE *Students' Right to Read* position statement asserts, "English teachers must be free to employ books, classic or contemporary, which do not hide, or lie to the young, about the perilous but wondrous times we live in, books which talk of the fears, hopes, joys, and frustrations people experience, books about people not only as they are but as they can be" (2018, p. xiii). Moreover, as the NCTE *Students' Right to Write* position statement states, teachers must foster student writing because it helps students to understand how their "language and ideas can be used to communicate, influence, reflect, explain, analyze, and create" (2014, p. xxi). With these statements in mind, I pinpointed areas within lessons to engage my students; to let them narrate their own lives; and to help them develop the reading, writing, and speaking skills that they need to be successful.

The unit I focus on here took place in a public high school in Brooklyn, New York. The school was grounded in social justice pedagogy with performance-based assessments at the root of learning. The classroom culture was designed with student voice at its center. I implemented this particular unit first in an eleventh-grade classroom after the grand jury decision not to indict Darren Wilson, the police officer who fatally shot Michael Brown in Ferguson, Missouri, and then adapted the unit for ninth graders by incorporating accessible texts for that group. The student population of the school was mainly Brown and Black. The school was organized around integrated coteaching. As I created the unit, I kept in mind different populations such as English as a New Language (ENL) learners, making particular adjustments within the readings, including making translations and audio versions available.

Framing the Issues

The unit was structured to provide students with a vocabulary to articulate their reactions and opinions. We started with the case of Michael Brown, which contains many layers that remain deeply embedded in the aftermath of his shooting. In the wake of the protests of unarmed young Black men at the hands of police across the country, the US Department of Justice launched its six-month investigation that identified multiple patterns of unlawful conduct within the Ferguson Police Department that violated the First, Fourth, and Fourteenth Amendments to the US Constitution. As we studied the case, the young people in my classroom began with a timeline of events that mapped out each detail as the days of the unit went on, beginning with the 911 call made from the convenience store regarding the robbery, the call that ultimately targeted Brown and his friend. I included a minute-by-minute reporting on the timeline from when Officer Wilson responded to the scene to the interaction between the officer and Brown. The timeline of events concluded with the dates of multiple protests held across the country, and finally, Wilson's trial that ended with no indictment. Large calendars took over our walls, as students each chose one event on the timeline and summarized it in their own words on large Post-it notes. We then pasted their summaries on poster-sized calendars to visually experience the timeline of events that spanned seconds to minutes to a year of injustices. As active participants in their learning, young people used their bodies continuously as they moved around our shared spaces; they took pride in being able to see their work come to life.

After creating a timeline, we began our study of the focal case, reading and analyzing social justice literature on critical, literal, and interpretive levels. We wrote critically and creatively to develop our own claims about social justice issues and engaged in meaningful classroom dialogue that spoke directly to our essential questions about community, literature, and social action: What aspects of my community help to define who I am? How can I take my knowledge about language, naming, assimilation, or Ebonics into the community? How can literature inspire social change? How can we create change in the world by turning our voices into action? How can different critical lenses affect our reading of literature? How can we use literature to reflect on our own growth and our contributions to the community? As we deepened our understanding of the issues that began with the case of Michael Brown, these young people made connections to other important cases and issues around the world, including but not limited to the stories of Aiyana Jones, Trayvon Martin, Emmett Till, Philando Castile, Tamir Rice, and Rekia Boyd. Through the use of social media and technology, which we brought into the classroom, these young people ultimately developed a platform and space in which they explored these topics and used insights from their lives to write for change and social justice.

Finding Voice through Personal Narratives

Through reading personal narratives, students found their own voices. The readings flowed: In addition to our anchor text, Ta-Nehisi Coates's *Between the World and Me*, students read official documents from Officer Wilson's grand jury testimony, including the alibi; Dorian Johnson's testimony, framed by critical historical news articles of the time and grounded by nonfiction works; selected excerpts from Bryan Stevenson's *Just Mercy* and Michelle Alexander's *The New Jim Crow: Mass Incarceration in the Age of Colorblindness*; and Kendrick Lamar's full music album *To Pimp a Butterfly*. Furthermore, we explored revolutionary speeches such as "The Black Revolution" by Malcolm X. As I continued to watch young people use the readings as a basis for participating in the ongoing social discourse, I continued to identify the pedagogical possibilities for critical English educators to do the work of ensuring that Black texts and Black lives matter in their spaces.

For those of you who may not have read the anchor text, Coates structures the book as a letter written to his son, who did not handle the news of Officer Wilson's non-indictment well. Written through shadowed voices of James Baldwin and Malcolm X, Coates encapsulates the feelings of oppression and the reality of what it means to be Black in America. Our discussion of the book led us to think together about the theme of the Black body and how protecting it, fearing its loss and its destruction, echoes through trying accounts of the "American Dream" and what it means to people of color. At the end, Coates offers his son glimpses of hope and understanding through platforms of taking action, remaining true to his identity, and not conforming to what the world wants him to be. Through their careful study of this book, students not only learned about the impact of oppression, but they also learned to identify a central claim.

The complementary texts I chose for this unit then allowed students to identify each part of an argumentative essay clearly through different mediums. For example, students made connections of effective counter-argument strategies through reading Officer Wilson's testimony against the counter-testimony of Dorian Johnson, Michael Brown's friend and the only eyewitness. By comparing these texts, students were able to make connections about the kinds of persuasive language that can be used to qualify two different perspectives on one incident, which then led them back to Coates's text. As they further drew connections between and among texts, they understood the severity of this very public incident, especially when Coates refers specifically to the case of Michael Brown. This unit equipped students with the relevant background knowledge and vocabulary as they adopted a new perspective on the case and its call to hope in moving forward. Making these connections also deepened their understanding of ELA because through these different narratives and styles of writing, students constructed their own stance and interpretation of Brown's case in relation to Coates's fear for his own son. Ultimately, my students facilitated seminar discussions of how the Michael Brown case influenced Coates's decision to write this letter to his son, while they explored the implications of the case within his writing, and even further, as they shadowed their own opinions, leading them to their final assessment of how injustices are viewed within their own lives and community.

I next facilitated a simulation for which I have compiled more than 100 names of unarmed Black and Brown people whose lives have been taken at the hands of law enforcement, a list that, unfortunately, I continue to add to and update every month. Lives taken by perpetrators held unaccountable. This activity was the start of a beautiful journey that my class and I walked together.

I placed one name on each card along with each person's age and the city and state where the incident happened. Below, I included three to eight sentences about the incident. Fast-forward a few lines down, and I placed the "outcome." Each young person received a card to quietly and independently read. I asked them to stand as soon as they had finished. As I watched eyes scavenge the card for an answer, flip to the backside to see more, and find nothing but a blank surface, I began to feel my own sadness take a seat within our shared space. When all of the young people were standing, I asked them to walk around and share the name on their card with a partner. I, too, took part in this activity and walked among the young agents of change. Very quickly, something magical began to happen. Third-person narratives transformed into first person as young people embodied the names on the cards. They each became the lost soul, and shared their story. Pairs become trios, as trios become mini-cyphers where students eagerly listened to the narratives of their counterparts. Words began to transmit across the classroom that resonated from one ear to another, words such as *no indictment, charge pending, family granted money*. As every young person began to want to meet every name, the truth sat at the pits of their stomachs of how each body had been unarmed, each body was a body of color, and each body had not received justice. I gave the young people the opportunity to further research their name to uncover more details. This name became their companion for the remainder of our time together. They took on the full responsibility of sharing that person's story with those who may not know. #SayHerName.

Crafting Personal Narratives, Persuasive Essays, and Plans of Action

We next moved to multimodal personal narratives that I began by asking young people to think of a time when they felt or witnessed an injustice because of race or class. Their task was to create an expressive piece that spoke on the matter. Each submission was no less than four or five minutes and was presented in class to their peers. I consciously included various options to choose from, such as writing a spoken word piece of poetry, creating a blog or podcast, choreographing an interpretative dance or rap, writing and producing a dramatic skit, creating an art piece (for example, graffiti, painting, sketch), or formulating a tableau. Each submission required a written component explaining the choice of subject and medium. I asked the young people to use at least two pieces of evidence from any text we had read in class to make connections to their piece. The pieces produced through this assignment were widely celebrated when we came together. Young people facilitated class protests, filmed and edited short documentaries, and expressed themselves through interactive art that spoke volumes. Their understanding of the literature that they discussed in their mediums expressed the connection that these young people had made with authors who looked like them, sounded like them, understood them, and most important, valued them.

Crafting personal narratives in this way connects with exactly how contemporary youth communicate, express themselves, and ultimately make meaning of the world around them. These practices may step outside the formal practices of literacy and pedagogy, as popular and relevant culture becomes a central site for understanding cultural change. Personal expressiveness keeps alive questions and relationships between experiences and writing. If there are struggles that students deliberate in their minds and see in the world, there should be no reason that they cannot express themselves openly in the English classroom. Personal expression leads to praxis within the community because it allows young people to bring their authentic selves into their work. The journey in becoming leaders for justice is twofold. First, looking internally allows young people to explore their personal experiences, assumptions about others, responses in situations of negativity or violence, and learned behaviors. Second, by identifying and then expressing through a narrative art form major influences and experiences that have shaped their understandings and beliefs about race, diversity, and difference, they can move to other kinds of crafting, including persuasive essays and plans of action.

The language used in the personal narrative segment supported students in persuasive essay writing. The texts I chose allowed students to identify each part of an argumentative essay clearly through different mediums. As mentioned previously, students made connections to effective counter-arguments through reading Officer Wilson's testimony against reading Michael Brown's friend's counter-testimony. Through these texts students were able to see how persuasive language can be used to qualify two different perspectives of one incident. Students were able to refute existing claims through these testimonies, which they were later able to link to *Between the World and Me*. Making these connections deepened their understanding of ELA because through these different narratives and styles of writing, students constructed their own stance and interpretation of Brown's case in relation to Coates's fear for his own son. This gave students a foundation for crafting their own persuasive essays. I gave students various options to choose from to construct a persuasive essay: Should all police officers wear body cameras? Should people in this country have unlimited access to various guns? And does police brutality change young people's perspective on education?

They learned the skills of how to identify claims, select appropriate evidence to back up the claim, use persuasive language, and pose counter-arguments through reading testimonies included in the trial, writing poetry about the case, and writing a personal narrative memoir in response to the loss of Black bodies around the United States. Students further expanded their understanding of social injustices by addressing issues of race, class, (trans) gender, and language discrimination through performance-based assessments. Plans of action unfolded when we became critically focused on unlearning patterns and behaviors from the past and were able to articulate voices that would bring light to situations for others. Students became determined to take action within their local communities. They organized a sit-in protest and created student-led workshops where they engaged their peers in this work; they created wallet-sized cards that contained information on their rights and phone numbers to reach in case of emergencies. Other students expressed their plans for action through long-term commitments to returning to the communities in which they live, to teach and encourage the youth after college. These plans for action within the community would be irrelevant if they were not coming from within—lived experiences that young people have processed, reflected on, and are now ready to act on.

Assessment

In this unit, students were assessed through low-stakes writing, formal essay writing, and performance-based assessments. Just as important, though, I identified that activities such as these that weigh on our hearts require built-in moments of reflection and light. Literacies that involve such a high volume of consumption will essentially promote individual freedom and expression. Therefore, before I assigned a performance-based assessment for this unit, I knew I needed to see how this was sitting with my students. To get to further know them, I invited small groups to my classroom during lunch, where students could be themselves, break bread, and engage in discussions outside of a sometimes high-pressure environment. In these moments, I either engaged or observed but mostly collected information on who they were and how they interacted. These observations gave glimpses into the lives of young people who may be guarded during class. Identifying that adolescents, too, are literate members of various out-of-school cultural communities means that we must look past viewing them as occupying seats in any class. I looked at my students in the greater sense of who they were and what they offered to the outside community.

What Matters

Our classrooms matter. Healing and humanizing classrooms matter most. With the goal of helping our community interrupt chronic systems of oppression, our classrooms need to become spaces of healing where all of our literature and writing is innovative and designed to explore foundational issues that ground race, class, and ethnicity, thus creating a language of solidarity. The ELA classroom must interrogate acts of physical and linguistic violence against Black and Brown youth and take them into consideration when shaping curricula. If there is an event that threatens the safety of young people, our classrooms need to consciously function to restore it. Acknowledgment is not enough; the consistency of addressing traumatic instances, such as those in Charlottesville, is imperative.

We can, we will, fight the power! However, it becomes more than fighting. It is about loving. It is about transforming the power through, first, reflection and understanding. It all begins right in our community. In the wake of the loss and murder of Black and Brown bodies, and the mass numerical percentage of incarceration, leading us to a time of a new Jim Crow, it becomes imperative that we engage in these questions and practices daily. It is important to not lose hope in this state of being; together we can transform the power. As a teacher-student team, you together must think critically about what you can do to engage in dynamic conversation around issues of policing and civil liberties that are unfortunately much too real-life daily situations for us all. By not hiding behind the blind spots of curriculum, we must be able to exist authentically, be able to heal, and ultimately be able to conquer this duality in which we walk. Young people must continue to have a hand in their own learning, through praxis, leading ultimately to liberation.

June 2017: A Classroom Conversation

Someone too recently looked in my eyes and as tears sat in a space far
   too familiar and comfortable, they told me,
-*Change the world that I live in.*

Instantly a silence overtook my tongue as I wondered how many people
    have once thought this thought
Had the courage to utter these words
Had the bravery to attempt to even ask because I for sure did not.

And as I wondered where the root of this comment came from,
And how I can sit and trace it back to generations of oppression and
    pain
Or conversations of agony and failure
To moments of belonging
I couldn't quite categorize the true meaning
To me,
It was a silent cry for help.
A vulnerable moment
An exposed request
An open request
An undoubtedly *hard* request
Possibly, an impossible, possible request

And as we occupy space in a far too similar world
Where Black and Brown bodies are far too disposable
We must take a step towards not fighting *against*; but fighting *for*
Equity, equality, justice, empowerment—

Anything that will *let us move*.

Let us move, to the country of Love—

I will live in the state Most,
Where the work is grounded
Where healing exists, occurring.
Depth lives here,
Where voices are heard
hearts are acknowledged
as full beings, carrying
trauma, carrying words,
stories
on every stand of hair
that is allowed to belong on my body
on every strand of hair
that is accepted on my body
on every strand of hair
that we wear

You will live in Empathy.
Where you can no longer tell me,
Go back to where you came from

Because you will have a learned understanding of my pain.
Where the water we wash with will run through the same rivers and
    streams
and for the first time, you will feel that same water.
Empathy,
where you will *realize me*
you wont like it.
Where you will *feel me*
you wont like it.
Where you will *understand me*
you wont like it.
You will realize however, this state of submersion
will ground you in Love's reality
We will thus engage in a relationship to wage the struggle for liberation.

Because everybody in Love is—

Feeling into your state,
Moral beings
Corresponding with other bodies
A revolution ignites
Affective Revolution
Where systems of pain become engaged
When we observe the suffering of others

Only then, does love become the motivating force for your liberating
    actions—

You will move to More.
Wanting *more*.
More for yourself and for others.
in More where you challenge
your dehumanizing ways in the first place
now identifying the trauma and pain that we've walked with.
True reflection thus leads you to your
action.
Brought us to vacation together in Compassion—
Here we lie facing the same sky
for the first time an acknowledged sky that we share

the sands feel twin beneath us
as each dawn comes with a new approach.
Everybody in Love is free

We will travel to Invincible—
Inevitable forces have put us on this land
to see suffering,
to learn in twilights
those lessons that have stiffened my body
kept it hard through years, never letting
it breathe
and now in Love, we exhale

To our allies living in Everything, Restoration, Generosity, Humility—
An integration of the younger generation
who never knew a President without color, an internet without #Black
    LivesMatter, who have only been taught to lead as young
men, young women who will cradle reality.
Who will discover ways in which they will participate
in the further transformation of Love.

The sun in Love spends its entire being, its fullness, its existence on
    showcase.
Its love, liberation and dedication to light on our hearts to brighten our
    path, so we can begin to embrace each and every state
as one,
each and every state not as a number or a color
but a betterment of who lives there, moves there, inspires from there

Reminding this love for the beings in Love, our own skin,
inexplicable affection
from the words of discrimination, hate, cruelty and negativity we stand,
    in Love—little to no protection

The sun allows for our growth
Sees us all as one,
we must develop this tendency

a world of darkness and pain, of no sun
is difficult to imagine—

why do we look to it, to be only for warmth
when it's so much more than light, it is in fact what we do with its form.

Reflecting on the Black Lives Matter Movement and Students' Rights to Read and Write

Take some time to reflect on these questions, either by yourself or with colleagues.

1. When was the first time you remember being conscious of race?

2. Reflect on the racial and ethnic composition of your schools throughout your personal and professional development, neighborhoods, and family. What are you bringing or not bringing to your classroom from these experiences?

3. How do you respond to traumas that are happening in direct communities within your classroom? What types of outlets are available for students to engage in this reflection both during and after?

4. What's the most important image or encounter you've had regarding race? Have you felt threatened? In the minority? Have you felt privileged? Are you able to be vulnerable with your students to share your experiences and growth so they, too, can have the space to grow?

5. What can you recall about the events and conversations related to race, race relations, or racism that may have impacted your current perspectives or experiences as an educator?

6. Reflect on the demographics of students in your classroom. How does your curriculum speak to each student's needs?

I will die in Mercy
where I will be seen better

Mercy
Where anger is no longer our crutch.

References

Alexander, M. (2016). *The new Jim Crow: Mass incarceration in the age of colorblindness*. New York, NY: New Press.

Coates, T. (2015). *Between the world and me*. New York, NY: Spiegel and Grau.

Faulkner, W. (1991). *As I lay dying: The corrected text*. New York, NY: Vintage Books. (Original work published 1930.)

Lamar, K. (2015). *To pimp a butterfly*. Santa Monica, CA: Aftermath/Interscope Records.

National Council of Teachers of English (NCTE). (2014, July 31). *NCTE beliefs about the students' right to write* [SRW] [Position Statement]. Retrieved from http://www2.ncte.org/statement/students-right-to-write/

National Council of Teachers of English (NCTE). (2018, October 25). *The students' right to read* [SRR] [Position Statement]. Retrieved from http://www2.ncte.org/statement/righttoreadguideline/

Stevenson, B. (2015). *Just mercy: A story of justice and redemption*. London, United Kingdom: Scribe.

X., M. (1965). The Black revolution. In *Two speeches by Malcolm X*. New York, NY: Merit.

Resistance, Reception, Race, and Rurality: Teaching Noncanonical Texts in a White, Conservative Montana Context

Melissa Horner

As a teacher who was born and raised Montanan, teaching in rural Montana, I did the unthinkable—I cultivated a curriculum that became the "talk"—and not in a good way—of the school and community. My curriculum supported a critical literacy (Wallowitz, 2008) ethos and cohered around texts such as *Americanah* (Adichie, 2013), *Birthright: Born to Poetry—A Collection of Montana Indian Poetry* (Susag, 2013), and an abundance of media texts (for example, podcasts, newspaper articles, film, and music) coupled with academic scholarship. I chose to teach an English class that interrogated concepts such as meritocracy, hegemony, and race as a social construct. I invited to the forefront the literature by and social inequities of people of color; I summoned discomfort and encouraged a willingness to learn alongside that unease; and I insisted that the students in my classroom— "even though" they were born and raised in rural Montana—had every right to read, write, talk, and *know* about the topics, people, and ideas I brought into the classroom, however distant and disconnected they first appeared to be.

NCTE's *Students' Right to Read* position statement speaks to this point when it states, "The reader is not limited by birth, geographic location, or time, since reading allows meeting people, debating philosophies, and experiencing events far beyond the narrow confines of an individual's own existence" (NCTE, 2018, p. xii).

As a practice through our units of study, my students and I exercised ways to better appreciate how we understood and participated in the world we live in. One of the primary ways we investigated our own understandings, subsequent biases, and actions was to be as transparent as possible in our own positionalities and identities. The following questions often resided at the center of our discussions and inquiries: Who am I? And how does that influence the ways in which I acknowledge (or dismiss), understand (or don't), and relate (or not) to stories, concepts, individuals, and groups of people?

Positionality and Context: Who Am I? Where Am I? Why Does It Matter?

The acknowledgment of my own positionality is important to note because I am writing about my pedagogy and students from a particular space. I was born and raised in a Montana city of about 30,000 people and was brought up in a divorced, alcoholic, working-class family that hunted and fished for primary sustenance; I identify as an able-bodied, heterosexual cisgender woman; and I check the census box for race somewhere between white and the Turtle Mountain Anishinaabe (Chippewa) tribe my maternal family is enrolled in and hails from. I offer these components of my positionality as a way to illuminate how I existed as a Montana "insider" who brought to bear on her classroom very "outside" ideas via my curriculum. One key distinction, though, between my students and me was class. I taught in an almost exclusively white, affluent, conservative, rural (population 800) Montana community. Class was often what created a barrier between my students and me—when we could meet in so many other ways, class differential was consistently present.

My students and I were raised in similar primary discourse communities (Gee, 1989), which is imperative to consider when noting the personal lenses through which each of us reads texts and applies them to the world around and outside of ourselves. When I consider many of the understandings and shifts my students worked through over the course of the year, I noticed that my own grappling, understandings, and learning journey were similar to theirs. I too didn't know Montana was considered rural on a national scale, or the implications of that label, until I was getting my undergraduate degree; I had never heard of lenses of any kind, critical or otherwise, until I was out of high school; and I didn't know that white people who were working as hard as they could for a living in rural

Montana had any sort of relationship—for better or worse—to larger cultural, sociopolitical, systemic issues of inequality. In short, many of my own prior unknowings mirrored those of my students. I found I could relate to my students in these ways, and I tried to lead with that vulnerability, along with broader, more complex understandings I have come to, through much of my teaching.

Curriculum: "We don't see things as they are; we see things as we are."

I teach ELA for grades 9 through 12, and I find inspiration for my curriculum from writer Anaïs Nin: "We don't see things as they are; we see things as we are" (1961, p. 94). Using this premise as an entry point, I organized the senior English class, on which I'll focus here, into four eight-week units. Each unit had a primary goal or focus and was designed to build on the prior unit's understandings and masteries, all by way of preparing the students for the individual research projects that would take place in the fourth quarter of the year.

Dedicated to discovering and applying critical lenses (Appleman, 2015) while reading William Golding's *Lord of the Flies*, I created opportunities in the first quarter for students to illuminate and discuss how meaning and interpretation might transform as they replaced one lens with another, or layered on lenses, as they read the focal text. The second quarter's focus cohered around Native—specific to Montana tribes—texts, primarily poetry, music, history, and current events. Alongside, and in application to, the focal texts, the students read and completed activities about concepts such as meritocracy, ethnocentrism, hegemony, oppression, and cognitive dissonance. During the third quarter, the class conducted a study of critical race theory (Delgado & Stefancic, 2013) and race and racism in the United States as a way to develop racial literacy (Guinier, 2004). Our anchor text was *Americanah* by Chimamanda Ngozi Adichie, which centers on Ifemelu, a Nigerian woman studying in the United States. Adichie uses this character and setting to shed light on race and racism in the United States based on a non-American Black perspective and experience. Throughout the unit, I wove in material about concepts such as racial microaggressions, redlining, institutional racism, and race as a social construct, along with examples of segregation and systemic racism in pop culture and media on a national scale, as well as local examples that often illuminated institutional racism toward Montana's Indigenous populations. For the fourth quarter of the year, I invited students to apply all that we had engaged in and gained knowledge about during the previous three quarters to generate their own (guided) critical research projects (Borsheim & Petrone, 2006). These projects began with the words of Zora Neale Hurston: "Research is formalized curiosity. It's poking and prying with a purpose" (1942, p. 143). With those words and the direction that their chosen research topic was to be an entry point into a larger economic, social, cultural, or political issue—many of which we'd at least touched on in the three quarters prior—the students then conducted in-depth research about an issue, concept, or topic of their choosing that mattered to them.

For the sake of brevity and in order to provide concrete examples of moments of learning and adjustment—for myself and the students—I focus primarily on the second and third quarters. In doing so, I illustrate instances wherein student discomfort, resistance, and unknowing need not be a catalyst to exclude controversial texts and discussions in a classroom, regardless of context, rural or otherwise.

Student Resistance: Navigating Negative Affective Responses

Over the course of the year, and on many occasions, student resistance to the curriculum emerged. The most common display of this resistance was in the form of negative affective responses such as anger, despondence, contention, and apathy. As I learned about my students while regularly reading about other educators who share their experiences of student resistance in the classroom (for example, see Wallowitz, 2008; Tatum, 1992), I began to adjust and tailor my curriculum to create space for the resistance.

I found three inroads that best served my goal of creating space for and normalizing resistance that was so often present in my classes. One useful way of going about this was to teach my students explicitly about cognitive dissonance, or "when a learner—any one of us—finds her- or himself grappling with new information in light of old understandings" (Gorski, 2009, p. 2). I folded this concept into our classroom lexicon while using the real-time understanding of it as a common language and tool to help recognize and navigate instances of individual and class-wide disorientation and dissonance.

A second way I was able to explore and transform student resistance was by teaching concepts such as meritocracy, hegemony, and oppression through reading about these concepts as well as doing hands-on activities that I developed—not unlike how one might teach grammar or literary concepts such as symbolism or foreshadowing. In doing this, I was able to compile the tools and language we needed to have as a class in order to unpack, discuss, and develop understandings about nuanced and often controversial topics.

The final and most powerful way that I engaged student resistance is through a practice my students came to know as *meta-moments* (Petrone, 2015). Meta-moments became instances wherein the students and I intentionally created a relief valve, so to speak, for any tension and emotion that occurred in our learning environment. Tension and challenging emotions often emerged as a result of the work we were partaking in that sought to make invisible systems and ways of knowing visible for critique and deeper understanding—which often caused disruptions in previous ways of knowing. For example, after a particularly grueling academic reading about racial microaggressions (Sue et al., 2007) and the subsequent discussion about how we might see microaggressions show up in our daily lives—from basketball games against neighboring Native reservation schools, to the most recent episode of *The Walking Dead*, to presidential campaign trail utterances—with about fifteen minutes of class left, I noticed that over half the class was either noticeably angry, agitated, or withdrawing from the conversation. At this point, the practice of meta-moments dictated that we cease having the discussion we were having and create a space to hover above—through talking or writing—what was happening in the classroom at that moment, so we created a meta-moment in time. In other words, at this point, we stopped discussing racial microaggressions and we began talking or writing about two things: (1) How am I feeling in this moment—what do I notice about the emotions I am experiencing as I engage in this discussion? And where can I trace the source of these emotions to? (2) What are we actually talking about when we talk about racial microaggressions (or whatever the topic at hand might be)? Another way of thinking about this question is this: What larger—or even, more personal—issues are underpinning the discussion, and how might *those* issues be related to how I am emotionally experiencing this conversation or topic?

In my classroom, meta-moments were almost always a writing exercise followed by discussion, if the students had the capacity and desire to engage in a verbal meta-moment with their peers and me. In participating in this practice over the course of the year, the students communicated that they were not only able to reorient themselves back to a place where they felt more capable of contributing to the discussion, but they also were able to create a productive space for introspection and further understanding of how and why they might experience what they do during challenging class discussions about hard topics, and how they might move forward in future readings and discussions.

I offer two examples of the power of this practice. First, during the racial microaggressions meta-moment just mentioned, one student wrote,

> I'm really angry right now. It's like me and all the other white people have to be politically correct every minute of every day so as to not microaggress [sic] anyone. What is new to me though is that just because I feel this way doesn't make the experience of any other person invalid. I didn't really consider that before.

In this instance, the student conveyed her sense of her own anger as well as her frustration with the way she felt was necessary for her to participate in society. Most important, she identified how her own engagement in and reaction to the topic related to others' experiences.

The second example occurred during a meta-moment we had after reading about and discussing racial identity development (Tatum, 1992). A particularly agitated student wrote for a long time, and the final line on his sheet of paper was,

> I never thought I was a race, and now that I have to recognize that I am, because society says I am, I am having a hard time swallowing that. Especially since that means I have things and know things <u>because</u> of my race, not just because of who I am. So ya, I'm pissed that no one told me this before now.

This student's meta-moment response indicates how new knowledge—realizing his whiteness is raced and therefore provides certain advantages separate from his own, known identity—is disruptive to his sense of self. His subsequent anger at having not previously had space and opportunity to be able to know and make sense of this knowing illustrates the work he is now doing to reconcile what he previously had thought he knew of himself, and the world he inhabits, with what he has now realized. After each of these examples, the students communicated to me—in writing and verbally—their willingness and commitment to continue exploring and fully participating in the unit of study, despite the challenges it was presenting and emotions it was generating, *because* they felt seen, heard, and validated in their experiences and processing during the class.

Meta-moments create a space that prioritizes and normalizes the emotionality of learning, reading, and talking about concepts, events, and issues that often cause cognitive and emotional dissonance, in a way that is nonthreatening. They also allow students to express real-time individual understandings, connections, and emotions that, often, there is no other space to do so in. Most important, meta-moments ultimately create opportunities to pause discussions—maybe for fifteen minutes, maybe for two days—and come back to them when the participants are better able to move forward productively, with less of the emotional affect that often causes stimulating, albeit difficult, conversations to provoke fear, withdrawal, and a definitive end to such essential conversations. One day after a meta-moment took place, a student came into class and, while making a mind-blown hand gesture, proclaimed, "You guys, my mind is blown; it's like we can talk about pretty much anything; . . . meta-moments are like magic."

Making Connections: Applicability and Relatability to and for Students

Early on in our reading of *Americanah*, a day after a class discussion about the attention to the function of whiteness we would maintain throughout the unit, I was on my way back to my classroom. It was just before the bell rang to start fourth period, and I saw a student—whom I knew but did not have in any of my classes—rush out of my room, while tugging a black sweatshirt hurriedly over his head. As I stepped into my classroom, already brimming with anxiety and anticipation about the lesson ahead, I scanned the room, and the eyes of one of my students met mine haughtily. I felt my skin go clammy and my blood pressure rise. The student was wearing a sweatshirt I'd never seen him don before—one that I knew belonged to the student who'd hastily left my room prior to the bell—one that I was sure he was wearing in response to our last class session together. The student's entire sweatshirt was made up of the unabashed blue, harsh red, and pointed white of the Confederate flag. As the student made eye contact with me and saw me see his apparel, he nudged the novel on his desk and cavalierly, but surely, let it fall to the ground. My eyes, my head, and my heart rested on the scene in front of me—twelve white high school seniors, all born and raised in rural Montana, one of whom sat in the center of the classroom in a sweatshirt proudly displaying a flag imbued with racist meaning, with a copy of Adichie's novel *Americanah* lying face-down on the ground next to his desk. It's important to point out that Montana did not exist as a state until nearly twenty-five years after the Civil War ended. Given this, it was hard to understand this incident as anything other than either an open protest to my curriculum, at best, or a statement of white supremacy, at worst. I was unsure in that moment what would be best and right, but I was certain I had no interest in publicly shaming the student who was presently wearing the offending sweatshirt.

For that day's lesson, I had intended to dive more deeply into the issues of race and racism and author positionality that had started to emerge as we had begun the novel. However, I elected instead to focus on the symbolic nature of hair in the novel while discussing the author's use of rhetorical devices. This shift allowed us, as a class, to avoid a potential shutdown of discussion and invited a less explosive but still productive discussion. Thus, the students and I bravely plodded through the edgy class period, and with ten minutes left, I wrote this prompt on the board—a meta-moment—and asked the students to respond to it: "I know we didn't talk about it today, but my sense is that class was tense (or fill in your own adjective here). Please describe your experience/any emotions you had during today's class."

On their way out the door, I asked students to submit what they'd written. Consequent understandings and revelations about being *rural* through the lens of this vignette readily revealed themselves. The students wrote largely about the extreme discomfort during the class period—though only one or two mentioned the sweatshirt itself—and many focused on a self-determined "knowing" that they are collectively perceived as "hicks" or "racist," often solely based on the fact that they're from Montana, a rural place. That said, some students lauded their peer's action, while others condemned it.

After some time passed, I followed up with the student who had worn the sweatshirt to class. We were able to have a frank and honest conversation about that day. He communicated to me that he was sorry for wearing it to class, and explained that his reaction was based on his previous experience with the couple of teachers he'd had who had chosen to bring issues of race and racism only briefly into the classroom and had done so in a way that created an atmosphere of shame, guilt, and insufficient discussion and space for emotions and experience to emerge. His most poignant statement was this:

> I've been told by teachers, and even some media, that I'm White, I'm privileged, and that I don't understand why. And they're right, I *don't* understand why, and no one has bothered to help me make sense of any of it, until now. When I wore that sweat-shirt, I thought this book and class was just going to be another case of beating us up about something no one ever bothered to actually teach us about.

The student's honest analysis of his actions made visible one of the ways in which rurality and rural places are an issue of social justice. Two thoughts occurred to me: "Why hadn't anyone yet 'ever bothered' to teach these students the complexi-ties and nuances of ever-present issues like race and racism as a concept to be learned, rather than a topic to be debated?" and "Why did this senior English class in a rural place unanimously believe they were perceived as 'hicks' and 'racists' as though it were a natural and seemingly inevitable thing?"

The reading and activities we did around conceptualizing and applying race as a social construct were influential in evening the dissonance and promoting authentic understanding of how systems of racism work. One student commented, "I just didn't know that race was basically invented to support racism. No one talks about that." The student went a step further and commented, "I wonder what other constructs were created to use on other people." When I asked the student to say more about the "other people," she responded with,

> Well, like we talked about the Youth Lens [Petrone, Sarigianides, & Lewis, 2015] and youth as a social construct, and now race as a social construct—what about us? Like us here in Montana and what people think about us; is there like a "rural construct" that causes us to be marginalized?

This was a prime shifting point in the class—as the students began to gain under-standing in and confidence to discuss and apply concepts such as social constructs, among others (for example, hegemony, oppression, microaggressions), they were not only able to see more visibly and speak more deeply about these concepts and their related topics, but they also began to see points of emergence and application in their own lives and communities.

Conclusion: "I've experienced so many emotions in so many days . . ."

This journey was the most intellectually grueling, emotionally taxing, interpersonally connective work I have done to date. One student shared in a unit exit comment, "I don't think I've experienced so many emotions in so many days at school before this class. But there was surprisingly time to work through them too for the most part. I wish there had been more of that while I was in school." This exit comment, among others, further illuminates not only the existence of emotions in the classroom—particularly an environment that invites students to engage in ways that might provoke discomfort and controversy—but also the need to acknowledge, respect, and create space for those emotions.

Whether it's around a Montana bonfire, on a city subway, or in an ELA classroom, when texts, conversations, and diverse ways of knowing begin to make previously invisible structures, policies, practices, and norms visible, students—and parents and faculty—have emotional reactions. When our understanding of the world and of ourselves becomes disrupted, we often feel disoriented, and our protective mechanisms rise to the surface to counter any perceived threat. There must be space for this emotionality to occur in classrooms or the opportunity to understand and learn deeply will never take root—the emotionality of learning and learning in classrooms are not mutually exclusive spaces. Reading is emotional. Writing is emotional. Talking and listening are emotional. Learning is emotional. When constructing a learning environment that promotes dismantling, discomfort, and dissonance, it becomes irresponsible to teach and speak only cognitively; one must speak emotionally as well, and work to create structures and tools that identify and support the emotionality of learning.

Reflecting on Interrogating Racial Privilege and Students' Rights to Read and Write

Take some time to reflect on these questions, either by yourself or with colleagues.

1. What structures do you have in place to support students embarking on the emotionally grueling endeavor of learning about, alongside, and amid controversial topics, varying perspectives, and diverse lived experiences?

2. How do you, as an educator, plan to be continuously mindful about your own introspection, reactions, and purpose of teaching content and concepts that invite a wide range of emotions—students' as well as your own?

3. When have you deeply considered your own (in)visible motivations for teaching normative or nonnormative texts in your classroom?

4. In your specific teaching context (e.g., geographically, demographically, sociopolitically), how might you consider and anticipate student, community, and faculty reception and resistance in designing curricula that invite critique and discussion of topics like race and racism and the myth of meritocracy?

5. With clear boundaries that support a zero-tolerance policy for racism, sexism, classism, and other isms, what might you do and say to best facilitate dialogic invitations for students to discuss and truly learn about complex, often controversial, texts and topics?

The emotionality of learning applies not only to students but to teachers as well; it is vital that teachers recognize that meta-moments are not only pedagogical—which is primarily what this chapter addresses—but are also a personal practice. For example, at the conclusion of the school year I had my own meta-moment and took time for introspection about how I was feeling and what I have learned from the students who participated in the work I had invited them to do. I asked myself one of the same questions I ask my students during classroom meta-moments:

> What are we actually talking about when we talk about student resistance (or whatever the topic at hand might be)? Another way of thinking about this question is this: What larger—or even, more personal—issues are underpinning the discussion, and how might *those* issues be related to how I am emotionally experiencing this conversation or topic?

What I ultimately arrived at in my own meta-moment is that perhaps the ways systems of schooling are constructed encourage teachers like myself to assume that in making pedagogical choices that create discomfort and controversy, the affective student responses that arise are negative, which is precisely how I initially perceived them—and combatted and labeled them as such. But perhaps the resistance and the affective responses aren't actually negative; maybe they are simply part of a complex emotional learning process. Furthermore, I have come to understand student resistance and affective student responses as not only *not* negative, but actually as encouraging, common, and generative signs—indications that the learning process is progressing effectively. Within this framework, the collective task then becomes about finding routes within the classroom to intersect, acknowledge, and expand the emotional literacy, via listening, talking, reading, writing, and understanding, of students and teachers—myself included—as a way to connect and step into literature and life more fully and deeply.

References

Adichie, C. N. (2013). *Americanah*. New York, NY: Anchor Books.

Appleman, D. (2015). *Critical encounters in secondary English: Teaching literary theory to adolescents* (3rd ed.). New York, NY: Teachers College Press.

Borsheim, C., & Petrone, R. (2006). Reading, writing, and re-presenting research: Teaching the research paper for local action. *English Journal, 95*(4), 78–83.

Delgado, R., & Stefancic, J. (2013). *Critical race theory: The cutting edge* (3rd ed.). Philadelphia, PA: Temple University Press.

Gee, J. P. (1989). Literacy, discourse, and linguistics: Introduction. *Journal of Education, 171*(1), 5–17.

Gorski, P. C. (2009). Cognitive dissonance: A critical tool in social justice teaching. Retrieved from http://www.edchange.com

Guinier, L. (2004). From racial liberalism to racial literacy: *Brown v. Board of Education* and the interest-divergence dilemma. *Journal of American History, 91*(1), 92–118.

Hurston, Z. N. (1942). *Dust tracks on a road: An autobiography*. London: Hutchinson.

National Council of Teachers of English (NCTE). (2018, October 25). *The students' right to read [SRR]* [Position Statement]. Retrieved from http://www2.ncte.org/statement/righttoreadguideline/

Nin, A. (1961) *Seduction of the minotaur*. Chicago, IL: Swallow Press.

Petrone, R. (2015, November). Learning as loss: Examining the affective dimensions to learning critical literacy. Paper presented at the NCTE Annual Convention, Minneapolis, MN.

Petrone, R., Sarigianides, S. T., & Lewis, M. A. (2015). The *Youth Lens*: Analyzing adolescence/ts in literary texts. *Journal of Literacy Research, 64*(4), 506–33.

Sue, D. W., Capodilupo, C. M., Torino, G. C., Bucceri, J. M., Holder, A. B., Nadal, K. L., & Esquilin, M. (2007). Racial microaggressions in everyday life: Implications for clinical practice. *American Psychologist, 62*(4), 271–86.

Susag, D. (2013) *Birthright: Born to poetry—A collection of Montana Indian poetry*. Helena, MT: Montana Office of Public Instruction.

Tatum, B. D. (1992). Talking about race, learning about racism: The application of racial identity development theory in the classroom. *Harvard Educational Review, 62*(1), 1–24.

Wallowitz, L. (Ed.). (2008). *Critical literacy as resistance: Teaching for social justice across the secondary curriculum*. New York, NY: Peter Lang.

Get this!

Chapter Six

High School Students' Rights to Read and Write as and about LGBTQ People

Lane Vanderhule

In the beginning of the school year, I typically spend time introducing myself to my high school students, and I include the fact that I am a Gender and Sexuality Alliance (GSA) adviser. Making a positive first impression on students is key to determining how the rest of the year will pan out, but introducing myself as the GSA adviser is a complicated choice. Many students are often not familiar with the GSA, so introducing myself in this way gives me a chance to explain what it is. I am careful to be brief with my explanation so that I do not turn it into an infomercial. Religion and conservative values are loud and proud in my district, and it is essential that my sharing information about the GSA in no way alienates or makes any of my students uncomfortable. It is my goal to remain a safe(r) and welcoming person for all of my diverse students.

I feel a great deal of responsibility when it comes to how I introduce myself to my students. Although I've always been clear about being the GSA adviser, I have not always been so open when introducing my personal life. During my first three years of teaching, I never mentioned my family. Okay, that is not completely true. I made sure to mention that I have a daughter. I never mentioned that she is my stepdaughter and that I have been in a long-term relationship with her mom. At the end of introductions, I felt inauthentic. But I was concerned about what it would mean in my suburban school district if I outed myself on the first day of class. I was worried about the students thinking differently about me. I was worried about parent complaints and job security. So, I chose not to. Without fail, as the year progressed, students would get more comfortable, and I would answer their questions that grew increasingly personal.

"You look too young to have a kid that old."

"Well, she's my stepdaughter."

Often, the questions would end there. Other times, students would question my marital status, so I would tell them I was not married—omitting the fact that, at the time, same-sex marriage was illegal. I danced around the questions until they were too specific to avoid. When it finally came out in one class that I was gay, there were a couple of surprised faces, a couple of murmurs, and one giant football-playing student who said, "My brother is gay. He and his boyfriend are going to get married on an island." With that, I was out, at least to one class, and I felt as though I could breathe. The consequence of coming out to my students was something that I imagined. I expected a negative reaction. I was prepared for pushback. In each class that I came out to, from then on, I received a similar reaction. I had let my fear of rejection allow me to underestimate my students. That said, I believe that my classroom became more inclusive once students discovered more about me. I still had students who were very conservative and did not approve of the queer community, yet I was able to make the classroom feel safe for them as well.

In my second and third years of teaching, I introduced myself as the Creative Writing Club adviser, the GSA adviser, and a mom. I still was not mentioning my partner in the opening days of class. I asked students about any preferred names and preferred pronouns, but it was not until my fourth year, which started about a week after my finally legal wedding, that I came out during my beginning-of-the-year introductions. I had two ninth-grade classes that year, with about twenty-five students in each. There was not much visible diversity; they seemed to be a homogeneous blend of white. I told the kids that I had just married and that I was the GSA adviser. It took only a few questions for the kids to figure out that I had married a woman. I received nothing but congratulations and positive reactions from the students. It was only much later that I found out what an impact that announcement had—I had two transgender students and one bisexual student come out to me within the first few weeks of class.

Now I was at a place where not only could I breathe, but I could *speak*. Moreover, because I could speak, I could make room for my students to speak. And they did. Within that year, students began openly and comfortably discussing the complexities of intersecting sexual and gender identities in some of the choice novels that we read. This was something that felt new and different for all of us.

The willingness to speak openly about sexual and gender identities blossomed during our discussions of the students' independent novels. Independent choice book reading played an integral role in my classroom this past year. I followed many of the tenets of Penny Kittle's *Book Love* reading program (2013). Using this reading program as a template, I ran most class days in a workshop platform. Each class period began with ten minutes of silent reading. Students chose fiction, nonfiction, plays, or graphic novels. My first-year classes were very open to the idea of independent reading since many of these students had come from middle school classrooms that offered more independence and freedom when it came to reading.

LGBTQ-Themed Books

I kept LGBTQ-themed books prominently displayed around the classroom. Along with the LGBTQ-themed books, I displayed books from a variety of authors of color, in addition to popular young adult (YA) graphic novels and classic novels. My intention was to provide representation of LGBTQ-themed books as often, and with the same frequency, as other kinds of books. What happened was nothing short of amazing. Students chose and read these books frequently and shared often among students. Word traveled quickly among students that I had several LGBTQ-themed books. The books *Beyond Magenta* (Kuklin, 2014), *Openly Straight* (Konigsberg, 2015), and *It Gets Better* (Savage & Miller, 2012) were the first books to catch students' attention. Students chose these books knowing there would be a time when they would need to share part of the book with the entire class through our book talks and shares. The knowledge that students would share their novels with the entire class did not deter students from choosing what some may consider controversial novels.

I gave students the option to share a single line, a paragraph, or a whole page while they sat at their desk or stood in front of the room. It was important to keep the process flexible. Students knew that if, on the day of their book talk, they only felt like sharing one line, that was all they had to share. There were other times when a student might particularly enjoy reading aloud and want to read more than one page. Requiring students to model reading for one another was incredibly effective in creating a strong classroom community. My participation in book talks was essential, and I shared my reading in the same format the students used.

As the year progressed, students shared ideas with increasing comfort and fluency, even asking one another questions about their books. Sharing choice novels and memoirs opened up a space for dialogues that might not have occurred otherwise. One particularly outspoken trans-identified student and another student who identified as bisexual led the queer-themed book talks. These students shared their books—*Beyond Magenta*, *Openly Straight*, and *Drama* (Telgemeier, 2012)—in a fashion that normalized the topic for other students. These students broadened the spectrum of what could be read in my class. It not only created a more inclusive atmosphere in the classroom, but also showed students that nonfiction, in the case of *Beyond Magenta*, is a valid and acceptable form of literature to read for an English class.

Social Justice Projects

We did a whole-class reading of *Night* by Elie Wiesel (1956/2017) right after an election cycle that was especially traumatic for my LGBTQ students. The tense political climate, combined with Wiesel's memoir, provoked conversations about how current political rhetoric echoed throughout the memoir in ways that I had not anticipated. I knew that my students had a lot to say and that they needed an outlet for their thoughts and opinions. A couple of my colleagues who taught Honors English 9 were doing a social justice project after reading *Night*. Their project was already in motion and was a bit more developed than we had time for at that point in the semester. I wanted to make the project happen, though, so I built the plane while I was flying it. After our daily ten minutes of reading, I asked the students to get out a half sheet of paper and write down ten things they wanted to change about the world. Their topics ranged from school lunches to the Syrian refugee crisis. The suggestions I offered included LGBTQ discrimination in the workplace, the wage gap, immigration issues, and voter rights.

After the students created their lists, I asked them to share with the people around them. After they shared in pairs or small groups, I asked them to revisit their original lists and identify anything they wanted to add or delete. After they edited their lists, I asked the students to choose a social justice topic from their list that they were genuinely interested in researching. I made it very clear that the topic needed to be something about which they were passionate or curious. I then asked students to choose large group, small group, or video as a format to share their presentations. Students overwhelmingly responded with a preference for presenting in small groups. We discussed how many resources their presentations should have and how long the presentations should be. The whole process took between fifteen and twenty minutes, and allowed the students to have active voice and choice when it came to these projects.

Students had three class periods to research and prepare for their presentations. Four students between my two ninth-grade classes chose LGBTQ-related issues. What happened with the groups was quite remarkable to watch. I did not have to redirect or censure any of the small groups. In fact, the three minutes I allotted to each presentation was not enough. Students actively questioned one another and were willing to share their opinions. The group that shared LGBTQ issues had the most difficult time getting through all of the presentations because the members had so much to share. Their group ended up creating a mini joint presentation and shared their ideas with their class.

After all of the students presented, I asked the class to share out as a whole group. Each small-group member had to share to the whole group something about one of the presentations that they found particularly interesting. In this setting, the students normalized the LGBTQ-related social justice projects. I say this because the students brought up and discussed the LGBTQ projects in the same manner as immigration, race, and the wage gap. The social justice project shed light on the issues equally and presented an arena for all sorts of students to share their concerns about equity and diversity. The dialogue among students made it clear they felt comfortable and open enough to talk about subjects that are often seen as too controversial for the classroom.

Reading Langston Hughes

Soon after the social justice project ended, we read poems from the Harlem Renaissance. The class had just completed a project on researching social issues that were important to them, and now I wanted to provide examples of how social issues influence literature. I made a calculated risk when I chose Langston Hughes's (1936/1994, p. 189) "Let America Be America Again." I was very aware of the possibility that students would make connections between a popular phrase of the 2016 presidential campaign (Make America Great Again). I read aloud while students annotated Hughes's poem. It was impossible not to hear the rhetoric of the current election echoing through Hughes's stanzas. The students muttered comments as I read the poem. I heard students whisper: Republican, Democrat, liberal, among other comments about the 2016 presidential candidates. After I finished reading the poem to the class, I instructed them to read it a second time independently. I told the students to analyze the author's word choice and tone. Based on the evidence they found in the poem, the students needed to answer the question, What kind of person wrote this poem?

Students annotated more quickly the second time around. They were quick to jot down notes and begin writing down their theories. One student, a young Muslim woman, thought the poem had inspired Donald Trump. She heard the narrator as an angry and aggressive speaker, a person who felt he deserved more. Another one of my students, a young white woman, identified the speaker as a young Black man who was possibly gay. The majority of the class agreed with her and could cite evidence and explain the connections they made to the poem.

Once students had reached the consensus that the author was a young Black male, we discussed whether Langston Hughes was gay. I mentioned how young Hughes was when he wrote some of his most well-known poems. One student shared that they were disappointed that a poem from so long ago, in such a different time, was still so relevant in their lifetime. Several other students also felt the disappointment. Another student shared that it was hard for them to believe that someone close to their age struggled with these issues so long ago. The poetry and the context resonated with this group of students. My classroom included students who were racial minorities, gay, of lower socioeconomic status—all students who rarely saw themselves reflected in the literature they read in ELA classrooms.

The next part of the lesson involved several more of Hughes's poems ("Theme for English B" [1936/1994, p. 409] and "Harlem" [1936/1994, p. 426]). I assigned each group a different poem and instructed the groups to read and annotate the assigned poem as a group. Students used what they knew about Hughes to analyze and pick apart the word choice in the new poems. After the groups discussed their poems separately, I brought the groups back together to share their findings with the rest of the class. Students made connections between Hughes's work and style and those of contemporary rap and spoken word artists. After completing this unit, I immediately regretted not seizing the opportunity to have students create their own poems reflecting their views on social justice topics.

Reading William Shakespeare

Shakespeare was the main subject in the fourth quarter of the honors and regular ELA ninth-grade curriculum. I introduced my class to Shakespeare through TED Talks, hip-hop lyrics, and sonnets. There was discussion about to whom Shakespeare wrote the sonnets and whether the relationships described were heterosexual or homosexual. Shakespeare clearly wrote some of the sonnets from a man's perspective to a woman. Some of the students questioned the gender of both the speaker and the recipient in other sonnets. They pointed to words in the sonnets that shaped their interpretations. Students grappled with word meaning, theme, tone, and authorial choices. They compared sonnets in an attempt to pick out more evidence for their claims about the meanings of the sonnets.

After spending time with the sonnets, we read *Romeo and Juliet* and watched the 1968 movie version one act at a time (Brabourne, Havelock-Allan, & Zeffirelli, 1968). After only a few lines into the play, the students realized that *Romeo and Juliet* is not as tender and romantic as most of them had envisioned. In the first scene, the characters engage in humorous dialogue about virginity, sex, and partying. Students asked whether it was appropriate to read or watch the play in a school setting. Similar questions arose when we watched the 1996 Baz Luhrmann version of the play (Luhrmann, Martinelli, & Luhrmann, 1996). The more contemporary portrayal of the play included sex, drugs, and partying in an environment that was more similar to the world in which the students currently lived.

Luhrmann introduces Mercutio in quite a dramatic fashion (Luhrmann, Martinelli, & Luhrmann, 1996). Mercutio is erratically driving a black sports car with an eponymous vanity plate, and he touches up his red lipstick in the rearview mirror. Mercutio then steps out of the car in a thigh-grazing sparkly mini-dress and high heels. At this point, it was necessary to stop the movie because questions were bubbling throughout the classroom and murmuring began to take over.

"Why is he wearing that?"

"Is he gay?"

"What's going on?"

"Are we allowed to watch this?"

"Why does he have a dress on?"

"Does he have a beard and lipstick on?"

I told students to remember that the Montague boys are going to a costume party as a way to soften the blow of the first shot of Mercutio. At the same time, I never wanted to overly explain why Mercutio has a dress on. In previous years students had commented on whether or not boys could wear dresses. My reaction was always to say, "Absolutely." However, the dress was not an issue this year. This was the first viewing in my class where not a single student commented *negatively* about Mercutio's clothing choices. The comments were inquisitive and not defensive. A couple of girls commented that they liked the flashy silvery cocktail dress that Mercutio wears to the Capulets' party. Another student, who identifies as a transgender man, said, "I'm strangely attracted to Mercutio." He then went on to say that he felt confused by how he felt when he looked at Mercutio. Many other students agreed. One white, straight-identified, LGBTQ ally football player commented that Mercutio had great legs. After the students saw Mercutio for the first time, a majority suggested that they wanted to be friends with him.

Romeo is not drunk in the play or in the Franco Zeffirelli film (Brabourne, Havelock-Allan, & Zeffirelli, 1968). In the Luhrmann version, Romeo is not drunk or intoxicated when he first sees Mercutio (Luhrmann, Martinelli, & Luhrmann,

1996). During Queen Mab's speech, it was obvious to most students that Mercutio is intoxicated. Mercutio dances toward Romeo and pulls an invitation from between his legs. Romeo rushes to calm Mercutio down. Mercutio brings out a tiny pill that one could assume is ecstasy. Romeo takes the pill and slides into a drug-induced haze.

At this point in the conversation, I asked students what they thought of this version of Mercutio: African American, in a sort of drag, bright red lipstick, offering drugs. There was silence in the classroom. I presented the question again, and this time I got some shrugs. One student commented, "I'd like to hang out with him, except for the drugs." I encountered zero pushback from the class, and not one single question about the distinctive directorial choices that Luhrmann had made (Luhrmann, Martinelli, & Luhrmann, 1996). I have to admit that I was shocked. I asked if they thought Mercutio was gay in this adaptation. The students responded with more shrugs. Students commented that his sexual orientation did not change the plotline in the least.

A student in each of my classes mentioned, upon first seeing Luhrmann's Juliet (Luhrmann, Martinelli, & Luhrmann, 1996), that she, or rather the actress, looked like Harry Stiles from the band One Direction. This led to a conversation about how the story might be different if it had been about two boys. I mentioned that maybe the students could write a type of fan fiction about Romeo and Juliet both being boys. The students quickly stopped talking about Juliet and Romeo. The conversation turned to the idea that several students, maybe eight or nine, felt the real love story of the play is between Romeo and Mercutio. The students mentioned that Mercutio and Romeo knew each other for a longer period than Romeo had known Juliet. The class emphatically expressed that they believed Romeo's reaction to Mercutio's death went beyond a typical friend's response to a friend's death.

Reflecting on Students' Rights to Read and Write about and as LGBTQ People

Take some time to reflect on these questions, either by yourself or with colleagues.

1. What are your preconceptions or biases toward teaching a more culturally inclusive curriculum? Do they include LGBTQ people? Are you comfortable with your own knowledge of culturally diverse and inclusive literature?

2. Taking risks and trying new curricula in the classroom is often paired with missteps and lessons that do not go as planned. How are you prepared to handle new challenges to your current practice of teaching? Are you ready to bring in new ideas and viewpoints, including those relative to LGBTQ people?

3. Are there teachers in your school who are already teaching LGBTQ-inclusive literature or providing safe spaces for LGBTQ youth? Are they successful? Could you reach out to them for guidance or collaboration?

4. What are some of the look-fors when it comes to providing a safe space for students in your classroom? Will creating a safe space for LGBTQ literature and youth alienate other groups of students? How do you plan on handling potential conflict?

5. What are some examples of literature you already teach that you could easily incorporate with more culturally diverse literature? What are some ways that these nonnormative texts can enhance the more normative literature that is currently a part of your curriculum?

Shakespeare, Hughes, Wiesel, projects, and a class library. The curriculum-related choices I made with respect to these classes were not particularly controversial or revolutionary. Still, I managed to provide opportunities for students to discuss topics and ideas they wanted to discuss. The classroom library and independent reading developed a community of readers who were comfortable talking to one another. The social justice projects encouraged the students to research topics that mattered to them. The discussions about Hughes's poetry showed the students that the issues and struggle they faced as teenagers are struggles that people have grappled with for years. The students chose to discuss love and friendship beyond the confines of gender and based their opinions on evidence from the film and text of *Romeo and Juliet*. I do not think that every student shared the same beliefs about the topics we discussed in those classes. I do not expect that to be true, but I witnessed students who were typically silenced speak out in the midst of a social climate that was telling them to be quiet. It is not lost on me that there are students who feel silenced in my classes due to the open and accepting classroom environment I create. I accept the fact that some students will not be comfortable to make racist, homophobic, classist, or other derogatory remarks in my classroom. I hope to create an atmosphere where even students with starkly differing views can still find value and feel valued in my class. I am not looking to change minds, but rather to provide opportunities for conversations that might not otherwise occur.

I will never know if my coming out to those students had anything to do with their speaking out in my class. I can't deny that there is a part of me that truly believes it did matter. It mattered to kids who have never seen an open and out teacher. It mattered that I was just a regular adult who happened to be gay. I can make many guesses about what mattered in that classroom. Something that I know for sure, however, is that magic can and will happen in a classroom when students and staff feel safe, supported, and heard.

References

Brabourne, J., & Havelock-Allan, A. (Producers), & Zeffirelli, F. (Director). (1968). *Romeo and Juliet* [Motion picture]. United Kingdom: BHE Films.

Hughes, L. (1994). A dream deferred. In A. Rampersad & D. E. Roessel (Eds.), *The collected poems of Langston Hughes* (p. 426). New York, NY: Alfred A. Knopf. (Original work published 1936.)

Hughes, L. (1994). Let America be America. In A. Rampersad & D. E. Roessel (Eds.), *The collected poems of Langston Hughes* (p. 189). New York, NY: Alfred A. Knopf. (Original work published 1936.)

Hughes, L. (1994). Theme for English B. In A. Rampersad & D. E. Roessel (Eds.), *The collected poems of Langston Hughes* (p. 409). New York, NY: Alfred A. Knopf. (Original work published 1936.)

Kittle, P. (2013). *Book love: Developing depth, stamina, and passion in adolescent readers*. Portsmouth, NH: Heinemann.

Konigsberg, B. (2017). *Openly Straight*. New York, NY: Arthur A. Levine Books.

Kuklin, S. (2016). *Beyond magenta: Transgender teens speak out*. London, United Kingdom: Walker Books.

Luhrmann, B., & Martinelli, G. (Producers), & Luhrmann, B. (Director). (1996). *Romeo + Juliet* [Motion picture]. United States: 20th Century Fox.

Savage, D., & Miller, T. (2016). *It gets better: Coming out, overcoming bullying, and creating a life worth living*. New York, NY: Penguin Books.

Telgemeier, R. (2012). *Drama*. New York, NY: Graphix/Scholastic.

Wiesel, E., & Wiesel, M. (2017). *Night*. New York, NY: Hill and Wang. (Original work published 1956.)

Chapter Seven

Asking the Right Questions: Bringing Disability Studies into the High School Classroom

Jeff Blair

When people ask me about my profession, I often state, "I get paid to ask questions." I'm only partly kidding with this playful response. I believe passionately that one of my primary obligations as an English teacher is to have my students consider the literature—and, by extension, their lives—in ways they might not have without probing. NCTE affirms the importance of giving students "freedom to formulate and evaluate ideas" (National Council of Teachers of English, 2014, p. xxi). For me, that starts with a good question.

Giving Attention

The problem with questions, of course, is that they entail an act of reduction. Certain conversations get privileged, which means others are neglected. As a result, important groups, issues, and topics never make it into the classroom, and there is no way around this reality. After years of teaching a literature class thematically devoted to voices neglected by dominant cultures, I became convinced that I was not asking all the right questions. I was neglecting a disability studies approach in the curriculum.

As with all of us, disability permeates areas of my personal life: my father using a walker after crippling, unsuccessful back surgeries; my sister struggling with mental illness that went improperly diagnosed for decades; my youngest son's early years relying on portable oxygen tanks due to lung issues that resulted from his premature birth. This extends to my professional life as well. Although I am a full-time regular education teacher in my high school, I work once a week in my building's Integrated Learning Center (ILC) for students with significant intellectual disabilities. I teach socialization skills to some of those students, and with others, I help them act out lines from Shakespearean tragedies, using literature as a vehicle for cultural understanding and for a greater sense of how to navigate their world.

Yet, when it came to the literature I taught in my own classroom, I didn't give the topic a thought.

This omission hit me one afternoon when two of the ILC teachers stopped me in the hall. They shared their excitement that one of the students was quoting lines of Shakespeare to them, which she had memorized after the acting we had done together. That got me thinking about not only the transformative power of literature, but also about how that power extends in multiple directions: literature is both transformative and transactional. I realized that, in not bringing disability into my classroom, I was enacting the same marginalizing that often occurs in society. Those without disabilities essentially dismiss those with disabilities or (literally and metaphorically) look away and go about their lives. We ignore what is in front of us and what is a part of us.

When I decided to give attention to disability in my classroom, I wanted my students to understand that just as disability is all around us in our daily lives, it is already present in the literature, but we choose to ignore it. Yes, there are numerous works of literature with the issue foregrounded, and we find them across genres. Courses devoted to contemporary literary fiction, for instance, can present provocative treatments of the topic, works such as Jose Saramago's *Blindness* or Mark Haddon's *The Curious Incident of the Dog in the Night-Time*.

For my class, though, I decided students should consider its presence in the more traditional texts that comprise much of the curriculum in my building. As Patricia Dunn (2016) puts it,

> Disabled characters are everywhere in canonical texts: Tom Robinson (and probably Boo Radley) in *To Kill a Mockingbird*; Lennie in *Of Mice and Men*; Laura in *The Glass Menagerie*; Tiresias in *Oedipus*; Doodle in the widely anthologized short story "The Scarlet Ibis," and so on. Classic texts will continue to be part of the curriculum for a long time to come, as well some of them should be. But teachers can take heed of how characters with disabilities are represented.

Disability is presented in literature more frequently than students—and perhaps teachers—might recognize. I wanted my students not only to recognize, but also to question and to consider carefully the implications of the treatment of disability in the works they read, works where they might overlook that it is even there.

Theory: The Three Questions

I decided initially on three questions that students needed to ask, three questions that would allow them to consider disability in a way that, I hoped, would do justice to both the literature and the people who have disabilities.

1. *What is the disability being presented? Does the text provide an accurate presentation of that disability?*

In *Narrative Prosthesis*, David Mitchell and Sharon Snyder acknowledge "the potency of disability as a symbolic figure" (2008, p. 48). Its "social and political dimensions" (Mitchell & Snyder, 2008, p. 48) are then largely overlooked. Instead, the text "binds disabled characters to a programmatic (even deterministic) identity" (2008, p. 50). To put it another way, the person with a disability is not explored as a flesh-and-blood individual with "voice and agency" (Dunn, 2016) and/or the disability itself is not presented as anything resembling a true condition. Rather, it becomes a metaphor for some larger meaning that we tell ourselves the author presents, but that, if we are being honest, we should more accurately acknowledge is the message the author and reader construct together, often from shared biases that we should question.

I believed the best starting place was the act of isolating the disability itself. My students do not have to be disability experts (their teacher certainly isn't) to work at identifying the condition and questioning whether what is on the page is grounded in reality or whether what emerges is simply a narrative contrivance to further the plot or theme, a contrivance divorced from any true experience. To be honest, I was less concerned with their ultimate answer. The power resides in the question itself. When they ask whether a character is being fairly presented, they are acknowledging that people with possibly different life experiences are an integral part of a world we all share.

2. *How is the character with the disability treated by their "normal" or so-called "typical" counterparts? How do you feel about that treatment?*

Disability is a social construct. Someone is only disabled in as much as others have decided what is "typical." Asking this question brings that reality to the forefront of students' experience. In giving attention to how the character is treated and to how they, as readers, feel about it, they move toward what Dunn calls a recognition of the "exclusionary practices in society [that] contribute to—indeed disable the individual—more than does that person's impairment" (2016). Questioning how the society in the text treats a character means considering how the students' society, and they as members of it, treat all people within it.

3. *What lessons about disability does the text offer? Is such a meaning important to your reading of the text?*

I wanted passionately to ask the first part of this question—it is, after all, the logical extension of the first two. Meaning, in my mind, suggests more than a sentence about theme that students can drop into a literary analysis essay, although admittedly they sometimes reduce it to just that. Rather, they should carry lessons with them beyond the classroom and into the world they inhabit and that they have the opportunity to shape. Also, in considering a message about socially constructed ideas of impairment and limitation, they give the topic a privileged position, one that a society steeped in ableism might not otherwise afford it.

I did not, however, initially want to ask the second part. I ultimately decided that I must, because analysis involves a necessarily personal component, where students should be permitted to form opinions and impressions. If we are serious about giving students agency in the construction of meaning, we must allow them to decide what is central to the text. The statement from Justice Douglas about "adventurous thinking" that opens our book, and from which the book derives its title, was actually from the Supreme Court's 1952 minority opinion. At that time, the majority went against Adler and decided in favor of the board of education. As the teacher, my role is at times, like that of Justice Douglas, to be the dissenting voice; at other times, my students will be presenting a different view. We are all richer for the exchange of ideas.

Using a disability studies lens means exploring "disability in the context of culture, society, and politics. . . . [It] presents a variety of perspectives on disability, from contemporary society as well as from a range of cultures and histories. It seeks to broaden the understanding of disability, to better understand the experience of disability in society, and to contribute to social change for people with disabilities" ("Disability Studies," 2014). My three questions and the accompanying activities for each allowed students to consider the text through this perspective. However, I recognized that they might ultimately reject such an approach. I could only invite students into the conversation and allow them to decide the extent to which it informed their larger reading.

Practice: Blanche Dubois and Gregor Samsa

The texts that I selected for my students are not presented here as the optimum ones for all teachers and students. To be frank, I picked these titles because they were already in my department's bookroom and on the list of approved titles for the course. Similarly, the way I addressed the three questions with these two works is in no way meant to be a prescriptive blueprint for how teachers must proceed. It is simply how I unpacked this rich and complex topic with my students. I hope it will suggest ideas for your classroom and texts.

Mental Illness and *A Streetcar Named Desire*

Tennessee Williams's Pulitzer Prize–winning play traces the victimization of Blanche DuBois, an aging southern beauty, who is ill-equipped to handle the brutality of the modern world, the cruelty of which is fully embodied in her brother-in-law, Stanley Kowalski. Her move from rural Laurel, Mississippi, to the urban jungle of postwar New Orleans forces her to confront painful truths about her past and her present circumstances. Ultimately raped by Stanley and rejected by her sister, Blanche is sent to the state mental hospital at the play's conclusion.

After we finished reading, I invited students to engage the first of my three questions by presenting the students with two conflicting interpretations of Blanche: (1) a quote from Williams suggesting Blanche was "broken" but "not mad" (Bak, 2009) and (2) an obituary for Williams's sister, Rose, that somewhat contradicts the Williams quote by suggesting strongly the connection between her mental illness and the author's characters (Viagas, 1996). The two interpretations raise the question whether Blanche has a recognizable condition at all. After some initial discussion of the differing readings, I presented students with a list of mental illnesses from WebMD (Goldberg, 2016). The students annotated the list for any descriptors that sounded applicable to Blanche either before or after the play's harrowing climax. As students worked through the list, talking with one another and with me, I discovered that a number of them were enrolled in my school's psychology course. They were more knowledgeable than I had expected about the nature—and accuracy—of the disability being presented, sharing interpretations of Blanche's possible post-traumatic stress, anxiety, or mood disorders that I had not considered.

When I was first designing the unit, I ran the list of mental illnesses by my colleague in special education because I wanted to make sure it accurately presented the information. She approved it and then proceeded to impress upon me the importance of *person first* language when discussing mental and physical conditions. As she explained to me, we do not discuss a *disabled person*. Rather, we refer to a *person with disabilities*. We must see people as individuals not defined by anything else, and the language we use, and even the order of our words, shapes that view. This principle informs my own teaching and writing, and it is important to impress upon the students.

The analysis of the play really took off when we unpacked the second of the three questions and discussed the treatment of Blanche and the students' feelings about it. To get at this question, I asked them specifically to write about the following: *In what way(s) (if any) is it troubling that she is being sent to a mental institution?* Some saw the action as appropriate and others as inappropriate, but almost without exception, they recognized the situation's complexity. A number of them pointed out that Blanche needs help but not removal from society. Several wrote from a historical perspective that in 1947, the year of the play's publication, mental institutions and the treatment of mental illness, as we know it today, were both vastly different; they viewed Blanche as condemned to a horrific environment. One student even noted the troubling point that, at least as far as we see in the play, "there was no definitive diagnosis before she was taken away." In considering Blanche's situation both in their writing and in the discussion that followed, the students were not only engaging in Williams's thematic concerns about the outcasts in society, but also thinking about the treatment of the mentally ill themselves.

This was no clearer than when we moved to the third of the three questions, and students began addressing the lessons about disability that the text offers. For *Streetcar*, this meant exploring how the play suggests the mentally ill in society ought to be treated. I had the students interact with an excerpt from "Blanche Dubois and the Kindness of Endings" by George Toles, which offers an interpretation of the most famous lines in the play. Blanche tells the doctor, "Whoever you are—I have always depended on the kindness of strangers" (Williams, 1947, p. 142). Toles sees this declaration as indicating "faith in an all-but-invisible clemency" (2009, p. 81). I asked my students to consider the implications of his ideas for individuals with mental illness in our country. They wrote about the needs for empathy and for support, recognizing the struggle that these people face. It made such an impression on them that, several weeks later, many returned to the issues again on a different writing prompt that did not even mention mental illness. For them, Blanche—and her removal to the mental hospital—ceased being another symbol in the play like the Chinese lantern, the polka music, or the frequent references to bathing. She became for my students a person with mental struggles, a person whose experience could mirror that of others in society, a person with needs that we could and should be considering for actual people in our lives.

Physical Disability and *The Metamorphosis*

There is little critical consensus about Franz Kafka's masterpiece. Gregor Samsa awakens to find himself now a literal vermin, a transformation that is never fully explained. He suffers feelings of guilt at what he can no longer provide for his family, and he faces neglect and even physical abuse at the hands of the people he loves so much. He is essentially punished for what is seemingly completely outside his control, and he ultimately dies from starvation. Readers are reasonably left with the question: What does it all mean?

Whereas with Blanche, we worked to see her as more than a symbol, Gregor presented a different opportunity. Gregor's transformation into a "monstrous vermin" (Kafka, 1915/1972, p. 3) is definitely and necessarily symbolic. In fact, on the day I introduced the novella, I provided the students with information from the *Gale Online Encyclopedia* (Franz Kafka, 2018). According to the entry on the author, "The oblique, allegorical quality of Kafka's stories has inspired myriad critical interpretations: his fiction has been variously described as autobiographical, psychoanalytic, Marxist, religious, Existentialist, Expressionist, and Naturalist. Most critics agree, however, that Kafka gave literary form to the disorder of the modern world, turning his private nightmares into universal myths" (Franz Kafka, 2018). I needed students to see that, with so little critical consensus, with so many lenses brought to bear on this short text, there is certainly room for a disabilities one. In fact, it seemed especially fitting to do so in light of Mitchell and Snyder's assertion that "disability characterization can be understood as a prosthetic contrivance upon which so many of our cultural and literary narratives rely" (2008, p. 51). Instead of seeing a person with a disability as a symbolic figure, here was a chance to see a symbolic figure as a representation for disability. And, given his tragic end, Gregor surely illustrates the treatment that so permeates literature: "the extermination of the deviant as a purification of the social body" (Mitchell & Snyder, 2008, p. 54).

As with *Streetcar*, we began with the first question, the nature of the possible impairment presented. We looked at a footnote to William Sokel's "Kafka's 'Metamorphosis': Rebellion and Punishment" (1956) where he references Clemens Heselhaus. That writer points out that Kafka suffered from tuberculosis and that Kafka referred to it as "the animal" (Sokel, 1956, p. 207, n. 8). Although both Sokel and Heselhaus see equating the vermin state to tuberculosis as being a bit reductive, we noted as a class that Kafka himself seemed to see his illness as a beast of sorts. I then introduced them to the work of Anthony Kraus (1999). He builds on the fact that Kafka was employed at the Workers Accident Insurance Institute, pointing out that with Kafka's law training, his work at the institute can be seen as his essentially being "an attorney concentrating on the emerging area of employee rights" (Kraus, 1999, p. 311). I informed students that, in his article for *The Labor Lawyer*, Kraus even writes a somewhat playful, albeit technical, hypothetical letter involving Samsa and the employee rights to which he might be entitled, including how he "may also have enforceable rights under the Americans with Disabilities

Act" (Kraus, 1999, p. 314). In learning this information, the students could grasp that there is an actual condition that can be attached to what is presented in the text, and that there is a logical basis for seeing the metamorphosis as symbolic of physical disability.

Having established Kafka's own physical and respiratory situation, I asked the students to consider the second question about how the character is treated by others. I had them respond to the following writing prompt: *If we read the novella as tackling the issue of physical disability, what is Kafka attempting to communicate about the experience for both people with disabilities and those near them? In what way(s) are people who have a disability marginalized?* This prompt might seem strictly thematic in nature (which is my third question). It certainly invites students to explore on that level. However, it is also inextricably linked to the treatment of Gregor, and their responses connected directly to their sense of his experience. The students had not yet completed the novella, not yet seen what happens to the "deviant," but they had read enough to be able to demonstrate a rich understanding of the exploited protagonist and the implications of his treatment. By looking at Gregor, students articulated how those with physical disabilities can feel guilty or burdensome. Several pointed out how physical disability alters the entire family dynamic. One student wrote how "those around [people with physical disabilities] commonly assume that they are unable to do something solely based off their disability. People with disabilities are also marginalized in that it can be difficult for them to describe the aspects of the disability to someone who doesn't currently experience one or never has." Another commented how people "tend to avoid [them] and act as if they were invisible in society." The chance to process on the page led one student to emphasize that individuals who have physical disabilities "do not have a lesser mind or set of desires" but can feel "trapped" by their external reality. In fact, in the follow-up full class discussion, a number of students grappled with this internal/external dynamic in play, considering to what extent our essence as people is tied to what our bodies can or cannot do. As these examples illuminate, writing allowed students to appreciate not only the character's specific situation in his literary setting, but also the often-dismissed feelings and experiences of a group of people in our own daily lives.

Since their writing about the character had allowed the students to think about at least some thematic implications, I was especially interested in how they would respond to the other half of the third question. Would they believe disability is important to the novella's theme? To find out, I had them briefly write about whether they felt it was responsible and defensible to read the text in this manner. Most did. However, I found myself surprisingly encouraged by the ones who expressed that they did not feel this was Kafka's focus. These students often felt like disability was only a part of much larger issues of mistreating people and casting them aside that occurs every day in our world. For me, even their act of dissent was still a movement toward empathy and away from neglect and exploitation.

Author quotes, excerpts of literary criticism, background readings about the text . . . it all might seem like an overly laborious process with the students, spending precious class time touching on these critical voices. Couldn't I skip over them and simply assign the task of reading the text from this perspective? The students could, after all, still participate in the same writing and discussion activities, possibly even arriving at similar conclusions even without the readings. A teacher might reasonably ask, Why bother with the outside texts?

My answer: In taking the time to legitimize the disability studies approach, I am giving power to such an interpretive reading, and I am also then empowering the students to join much more fully in the act of making meaning. Larry Scanlon first introduced me to Kenneth Burke's parlor metaphor, and *The Language of Composition* gives a wonderful modernizing of it, highlighting the notion that argument involves a response to the views of others (Shea, Scanlon, Dissin Aufses, & Harowitz Pankiewicz, 2013, p. 145). Like a parlor conversation, argument is a civilized activity that involves not simply spouting opinions, but, first and foremost, listening to the views of others before interacting meaningfully with them. Appropriating that metaphor, I would suggest that it is worthwhile to allow students into a parlor that they may not have previously entered. When we take the time to read these critical voices, my classroom becomes a space where students can understand positions about disability that they might not otherwise have considered, and where they learn about arguments to which they can eventually respond. It becomes a parlor where the marginalized are effectively returned to the center of the conversation.

The Fourth Question

My responsibility as a teacher is, as I have said, to ask good questions, and I quickly realized that there is a fourth question I had not considered when first mapping out my lessons. It is a question I should have known to ask (or should have at least been aware that the students were asking). It is a question that arises whether we give actual voice to it or not, so I believe it is important to share.

It came to me in the middle of our discussion of *Streetcar*. The students were especially focused, more so than usual, and even students who rarely participate were weighing in about the treatment of Blanche and its implications. There was an energy in the room I don't often see in a morning class, and I couldn't figure out why. On the spur of the moment, I asked the class how many of them had personal experience with mental illness either in their own lives or in the lives of people they know. When three-quarters of the class raised their hands, I realized why they were so invested.

I experienced a similar level of engagement when tackling physical disability with *Metamorphosis*. A student with Crohn's disease shared his experience being "confined to a wheelchair in the past," and I had no idea about this aspect of his life. Another wrote with vulnerability about the guilt and challenges he faces when interacting with a relative who has Parkinson's disease, and another reflected on her frustrations about how her brother with Down syndrome gets treated outside the home.

As their honesty bears out, our students live with disability themselves. They know people who live with it. They recognize the presence of it around them. And I found myself connecting with them on a deeper level as I saw how much their experiences with disability echoed—and even enriched my personal understanding of—my own. When we allow students to read, write, and discuss it, we permit them to clarify, refine, solidify, and even question their (and our own) thinking. And, at least to a small extent, we normalize both conversations and people that are too often ignored.

4. *How is disability part of your life?*

That is the question I forgot to ask my students, but they began asking it of themselves the moment I introduced the topic. In taking a disability studies approach, that question became acceptable and relevant, and the literature became less an artifact of the past and more an invitation to consider the present.

All four of these questions together provoked important dialogue, and my hope is that you use them as springboards for reading and writing opportunities in your own classrooms as well. These opportunities are not simply rewarding for teachers and students. They are essential.

Reflecting on Disability Studies and Students' Rights to Read and Write

Take some time to reflect on these questions, either by yourself or with colleagues.

1. All four questions discussed in this chapter are valuable, but consider the fourth one specifically: How is disability part of your life? Explore your response on both personal and professional levels.

2. Look over the students you have in your classroom this year. What disabilities are present in your room? How might students with these disabilities as well as their "typical" peers benefit from a disability studies approach?

3. What works of literature already in your curriculum (or available in your bookroom or library) present characters with disabilities? How do those representations affirm or challenge your own knowledge-of, and experiences with, disability?

4. How do the representations of disability in your curriculum connect to themes you already discuss? What new thematic possibilities does the presentation of disability provide?

5. According to this chapter, in our classrooms "certain conversations get privileged, which means others are neglected. As a result, important groups, issues, and topics never make it into the classroom" (this text, p. 78). If disability does not enter into your classroom conversations, what do you feel could be lost?

References

Bak, J. S. (2009). A streetcar named desire: Tennessee Williams and the semiotics of rape. *Tennessee Williams Annual Review*. Retrieved from www.tennesseewilliamsstudies.org

Disability studies. (2014). In *Britannica School* [Database]. Retrieved from school.eb.com/levels/high/article/disability-studies/609333

Dunn, P. (2016, August 29). Fictional characters with disabilities—What message do they send? [Blog post]. Retrieved from blogs.ncte.org/index.php/2016/08/fictional-characters-disabilities-message-send/

Franz Kafka. (2018). In *Gale Online Encyclopedia*. Detroit, MI: Gale. Retrieved from http://link.galegroup.com/apps/doc/H1410000032/LitRC?u=auro90272&sid=LitRC&xid=8c4b52c7

Goldberg, J. (Rev.). (2016, July 26). Types of mental illness. *WebMD*. Retrieved from www.webmd.com/mental-health/mental-health-types-illness#1

Kafka, F. (1986). *The metamorphosis*. (S. Corngold, Trans.). New York, NY: Bantam Books. (Original work published 1915)

Kraus, A. (1999). Assessing Mr. Samsa's employee rights: Kafka and the art of the human resource nightmare. *Labor Lawyer, 15*(2), 309–19. Retrieved from http://www.jstor.org/stable/40862673

Mitchell, D. T., & Snyder, S. L. (2008). *Narrative prosthesis: Disability and the dependencies of discourse*. Ann Arbor, MI: University of Michigan Press.

National Council of Teachers of English (NCTE). (2014, July 31). *NCTE beliefs about the students' right to write* [*SRW*]. Retrieved from http://www2.ncte.org/statement/students-right-to-write/

Shea, R., Scanlon, L., Dissin Aufses, R., & Harowitz Pankiewicz, M. (2013). *The language of composition: Reading, writing, rhetoric* (2nd ed.). Boston, MA: Bedford/St. Martin's.

Sokel, W. (1956). Kafka's "Metamorphosis": Rebellion and punishment. *Monatshefte, 48*(4), 203–14. Retrieved from http://www.jstor.org

Toles, G. (2009). Blanche Dubois and the kindness of endings. In H. Bloom (Ed.), *Tennessee Williams's a streetcar named desire* (pp. 61–82). New York, NY: Chelsea House.

Viagas, R. (1996, Sept.10). Rose Williams, sister and muse of Tennessee, dies at 86. *Playbill*. Retrieved from www.playbill.com

Williams, T. (1947). *A streetcar named desire: With an introd. by the author*. New York, NY: New American Library.

Part III
Supporting the Work of Teachers

An Interview with Angie Thomas

Mollie V. Blackburn

Sometimes I (this is Mollie writing here) take independent studies with myself. They revolve around some question or theme, provoked by some life event. They are typically informed by books, very often YA literature, but not always. Usually I'll start with one book, which leads me to another. Sometimes one book makes me want to read another book by the same author; other times one book mentions another; still other times, one author writes a blurb for another author, and that helps me get to the next book. The exploration is complemented by the discussions I share with friends about one or more of the books. I pose questions, listen to their answers, and articulate my thinking by answering my friends' questions. We offer each other recommendations, which keeps me reading and studying. Sometimes the books don't actually end up addressing my driving question, but they always inform it, and the question, of course, evolves. (It's my own independent study. I have some flexibility.)

The 2016 election provoked one such independent study. I was devastated by the results. The morning after, I stopped by a sandwich shop to pick up breakfast. The woman working there asked me how I was doing, and I burst into tears. No lie. I am a white woman. The woman was Black. I reflected on this moment repeatedly, with humility if not outright humiliation, as I read the news about more than half of white women voting for the candidate I not only did not support but vehemently opposed. My reflections continued as I read social media posts about Black women being tired of white women's tears, of white fragility, and I already knew it was no good to expect people of color to educate me on the ways I carry with me racist practices from being raised white in a society founded on the insidious fiction of white supremacy. It was time for yet another independent study. The theme was something about what racial revolutionaries look like, what antiracist allies look like, what microaggressions look like, particularly as represented by people of color.

NCTE's Annual Convention came right after the election, as it always does. Andrew Aydin and Nate Powell spoke at a breakfast I attended. They talked about their work with John Lewis in creating *March*, a black-and-white graphic trilogy representing the US Civil Rights Movement. These three books started the list, even though they were created by a racially diverse team, not only people of color. As I read and discussed these books with a colleague, Pat Enciso, she recommended Lila Quintero Weaver's *Darkroom*, also a black-and-white graphic memoir set in the South during the Civil Rights Movement, but from an Argentinian perspective. It describes some of the same events portrayed in the *March* books, from a different perspective. It was fascinating in that way, but I was ready for something more contemporary.

At the same convention, Ta-Nehisi Coates spoke. He read from *Between the World and Me*. Listening, I knew I needed more. I added his book to my list. He also talked about his work writing *The Black Panther* with Brian Stelfreeze, and this too went on the list. Jason Reynolds was also at this convention. I saw him on a panel of authors, where he was perfectly inspiring with both his insight and his generosity. My friend Courtney Johnson and I were talking about that, and she said I really needed to read the book he wrote with Brendan Kiely, *All American Boys*. I recalled that Cathy Fleischer had already recommended this one. I added it to my list.

December, January, and February, I read, read, read these books. And that's when Angie Thomas's *The Hate U Give* came out. That's when I got the chance to meet Starr Carter and watch her become a revolutionary. And that's when I had the chance to see the many, many ways her white friends failed her but also how her boyfriend, Chris, tried to do better, sometimes failing, but sometimes getting it right. So, when Angie Thomas, creator of Starr Carter, was invited as a luncheon speaker for NCTE's Conference on English Education, I was thrilled. Thomas reflected on her experiences as a student in classrooms. She talked about the teachers who meant well but missed the mark and how they provoked her to prove her brilliance. She talked about the teachers who meant well and did right by her and how they inspired her to shine. So, when the teacher-author-artists in this book and I had the chance to interview her for this book, we were thrilled. Arianna Talebian, in particular, wrote this:

> I cannot tell you how incredibly excited I am that Angie Thomas is going to write a piece! OH MY GOODNESS. I am currently reading *The Hate U Give* with my 9th graders through our BLM unit and it has been just surreal! The writing pieces that have come from her work are incredibly powerful. Just last week, for Dia de Los Muertos, I had my students write *ofrendas* from Starr to Khalil [main characters in her book] after the horrific shooting, then they wrote odes to their lost loved ones and victims of police brutality.

I have had much to learn from Angie Thomas, as have teachers in and beyond this book, as have their students, as Arianna points out.

In this interview, Angie Thomas talks about seeing power in young people, power in teachers, and power in students in relation to teachers. She talks about the importance of teachers challenging students who are in some ways privileged to interrogate their privileges, and affirming the experiences of students who are in some ways marginalized so that they might love themselves as they change their worlds. She talks about how this challenging and affirming might happen through the act of reading the same book. Students deserve this. They have the right to it. And with that, I hope you—readers, too—are thrilled to read our interview with Angie Thomas. . . .

Mollie Blackburn: NCTE's position statement titled *The Students' Right to Read* proclaims that "youth is the age of revolt" (National Council of Teachers of English, 1981, p. 3). This line brings to mind Starr Carter. What insights can Starr Carter and you offer high school students about being in the "age of revolt"?

Angie Thomas: I would remind them that they aren't too young to cause change. So often, adults make them feel as such, but they are in fact some of the most powerful people in the world. Marketers pay millions, maybe even billions, to figure out what appeals to them. They've created cultures—hip-hop is the most profitable music genre in the world, and it was created by teens. That's power. So never, ever think that your age limits you. You're not just the future, you're the powerful present.

Mollie: NCTE's *Students' Right to Write* position statement claims that teachers' feedback "should avoid indoctrination because of personal beliefs and should be respectful of both the writer and his/her ideas, even those with which the teacher disagrees" (NCTE, 2014, p. xxi). As a writer, who are the teachers who helped you and hindered you in your journey to becoming a writer? How did they help you? Hinder you? What did they do, or not do, when it came to your writing about topics that might be understood by some as contentious?

Angie: It's hard for me to say that any of my teachers hindered me in my journey to become a writer. Even the ones who meant well, but may not have said the right things only fueled me to push forward. The teachers who helped the most were the ones who introduced me to writers and works I could identify with, therefore helping me see that it was possible for someone like me to be a writer. One of my college professors stands out the most. He was the one who encouraged me to write about a neighborhood like mine—there are stories there that deserve to be told, so why don't I tell them?

Mollie: Jonna Perrillo wrote a blog post in response to NCTE's *Students' Right to Read* that "teachers' willingness to address controversial subjects has waxed and waned over time, but it has been consistently low since the 1980s" (2018). From your perspective, are there any costs of teachers and students *not* engaging in controversial conversations in their classrooms? If you could sit down with teachers, what would you tell them about this? What inspiration might you give to teachers wavering on whether to do this sort of work?

Angie: I need more teachers to be aware of the fact that the controversial topics they are afraid to discuss are things that are actually happening in some of their students' lives. If not their students, they are things happening in the lives of a young person who could be their student. By avoiding these conversations, we're telling kids who experience those things that our comfort is more valuable than their life, because essentially, that's what it comes down to—we don't discuss things because they make us uncomfortable. If we don't discuss these things, we end up with young people who are unaware of what's happening in the lives of people unlike them or who feel as if they don't have a "seat at the table." Let's not repeat the mistakes of the past. The young people you teach now will lead society one day. Allow them to leave their comfort zones now so we don't end up with leaders who operate in ignorance.

Mollie: Teachers who have written for this book show readers how they

- had their journalism students writing about immigrant families in ways that have material consequences for those families;

- fostered reading and writing among their linguistically diverse students;

- honored Muslim identities—their own and those of their students;

- engaged their students in the Black Lives Matter movement;

- taught their rural students to interrogate power dynamics, even those that seem far from their daily experiences;

- invited and facilitated students to discuss the lives of LGBTQ people with complexity and respect; and

- provoked students to explore how disability—physical disabilities as well as mental illness—is part of their lives.

What are some of your favorite books for young adults that might complement efforts such as these?

Angie: It's honestly hard for me to narrow this down to a few books, so instead, I would encourage teachers to check out the OurStory app by We Need Diverse Books. It connects educators with diverse books that address all of these topics and then some.

As many readers of this book may know, We Need Diverse Books is a "grassroots organization of children's book lovers that advocates essential changes in the publishing industry to produce and promote literature that reflects and honors the lives of all young people" (We Need Diverse Books, 2019). The mission of the organization is to put "more books featuring diverse characters into the hands of all children" (We Need Diverse Books/About, 2019). The organization defines diversity broadly, much like it is conceptualized in this book, to include "LGBTQ-IA, Native, people of color, gender diversity, people with disabilities, and ethnic, cultural, and religious minorities" (We Need Diverse Books/About, 2019).

Angie Thomas mentions the OurStory app in particular, which is described as a "book discovery tool" (2017). The app works like this: Student-readers, teachers, or librarians sign up through either their free membership for young readers or a paid membership. You're then guided through answering a series of questions about your interests—from reading level (for example, picture books, middle grades) to genre (autobiography, fantasy, graphic novel, and more) to identities and experiences (for example, disability, diverse family structure, racial or ethnic identity) to story elements (outcasts, travel, music, animals, and more). The app ultimately identifies "books with diverse content and by content creators from marginalized communities" (OurStory, 2017) that fit your interests. It is a resource that might be of use as you strive to engage in the kind of adventurous and revolutionary teaching advocated for throughout this book.

References

National Council of Teachers of English (NCTE). (1981). *The students' right to read* [Position Statement, rev. 2009]. Urbana, IL: National Council of Teachers of English.

National Council of Teachers of English (NCTE). (2014, July 31). *NCTE beliefs about the students' right to write [SRW]* [Position Statement]. Retrieved from http://www2.ncte.org/statement/students-right-to-write/

National Council of Teachers of English (NCTE). (2018, October 25). *The students' right to read [SRR]* [Position Statement]. Retrieved from http://www2.ncte.org/statement/right toreadguideline/

OurStory. (2017). We Need Diverse Books. Retrieved from http://www.diversebooks.org/ourstory/

Perrillo, J. (2018, September 29). More than the right to read [Blog post]. Retrieved from http://www2.ncte.org/blog/2018/09/more-than-the-right-to-read-2/

We Need Diverse Books. (2019). Retrieved from https://diversebooks.org

Protecting Your Students' Rights to Read and Write and Yours to Teach

Chapter Nine

Millie Davis

> *So, students' rights to write and read serve as a catalyst to think about . . . our teaching—not just curriculum, not just pedagogy, but the thinking, talking, and listening that we as ELA teachers do together with our students . . .*
>
> —Jonna Perrillo, "More Than the Right to Read"

As Jonna Perrillo suggests, do plan your curriculum and make your text choices to foster reading, writing, thinking, and talk. *Then* take proactive steps to protect these most important activities for your students and their learning. But know where to turn if you're challenged. While basing your curricular choices and classroom activities on NCTE's *Students' Right to Read (SRR)* and *Students' Right to Write (SRW)* statements, you should at the same time be aware of and consider the rules and procedures school districts have in place and that, as an employee, you need to follow.

Know and Follow Your School Policies

In a 2016 survey of NCTE INBOX readers, 41 percent of respondents stated that their selection of materials was guided by an informal policy, 29 percent stated that decisions were guided by a formal policy, and the rest stated that their school district had no policy or they didn't know whether there was a policy. Don't be among those who don't know about your district's policies.

Most school districts have school board policies governing how curriculum and texts are chosen. While the board has to approve these selections, they often cede the selection process to teachers or administrative committees. Often there are also provisions for supplemental texts. In addition, most school districts have policies on teaching controversial materials and on reconsidering texts. Only a few districts have policies concerning student writing. You'll usually find the policies on the district website under "school board" and "school board policies" and then under "curriculum" or "instruction" and sometimes under "parent/community relations." You may have to dig a bit, but do know those policies—for two reasons. First, know the policy so you can follow it in the selection of materials and methods for your classroom. Second, know the policy so you can at least notice where and when it's not being followed—for example, if a parent goes straight to a school board meeting to complain about a text or method you're using in your class instead of coming to you first. (See the model procedure spelled out in *SRR* under "Defending the Texts" [NCTE, 2018, p. xvi].)

Keeping People Informed and Building Buy-In

Beyond knowing the district policies, make sure to keep others in the loop about how you are teaching reading and writing—especially if you're including activities and texts that may seem controversial. Open your door and share with your colleagues, the principal, and parents about *what you're doing in your class and why*. You don't need to be super specific. Something important to remember, as Emily Knox's *Book Banning in 21st-Century America* points out, is that challengers often just want to be heard, and they don't really understand the reading process as we do. So help them understand. Jennifer Buehler offers suggestions for making colleagues and parents your allies in Chapter 7 of her book *Teaching Reading with YA Literature: Complex Texts, Complex Lives*. One example is starting reading groups for parents or colleagues to familiarize them with YA novels and the depth these stories provide for student learning. Penny Kittle has a great way of notifying parents about what she's doing in her class and explains a bit about how she teaches reading and writing in her "Letter to Parents about Reading and Writing." She begins her letter by saying, "A central goal of Writing is to establish a reading habit in the busy lives of seniors in high school" (Kittle, n.d.). She goes on in detail, explaining all the methods she'll use to help students develop that reading habit. Get buy-in from stakeholders, or ask yourself what you're willing to risk without it. Jeff Kaplan, former chair of the NCTE Standing Committee against Censorship, spells out how to do this in his blog (Kaplan, 2016). He lists all the people in the school and community whom we should let know what we're teaching, how, and why. What you say depends on who you're talking to—sometimes you'll be explaining a method as Kittle does, and sometimes you'll be talking about specific texts.

But even the best laid plans do occasionally go awry.

What to Do When Challenges Arise

If the challenge comes, and you need help, contact NCTE through the Intellectual Freedom Center (http://www2.ncte.org/resources/ncte-intellectual-freedom-center/): use the Report A Censorship Incident form (https://secure.ncte.org/forms/reportcensorship) or email to intellectualfreedom@ncte.org.

Although there are many organizations that deal with challenges to reading and writing in schools, they are not all equal in terms of the help and insight they can provide, their methods for doing so, and *their understandings of reading and writing in terms of English language arts curriculum and instruction.* Many resource books about censorship provide lists of organizations that work with challenges, but they don't do any more than that—leaving a person who needs help with a list to pick from at random.

Chutzpa or not, we at NCTE are the best door for people to walk through when they have a problem. We understand reading and writing in terms of ELA curriculum and instruction. We know and regularly work with all the other First Amendment organizations. We rarely try to solve the problem alone, but do so with those organizations whose expertise can help.

NCTE bases its responses to challenges on

- procedures—what the district policies say about curriculum, texts, and instruction;
- whether the procedures have been followed;
- the value of the text—we have ready-made, adaptable rationales for hundreds of books and a form to create your own rationale; and most important,
- NCTE beliefs about good curriculum and instruction in English language arts.

We keep private our interactions with teachers who have been challenged unless the challenge is already public knowledge because it's been broadcast in the media. Two examples:

- When Cissy Lacks was fired from the Ferguson-Florissant School District for letting her students use profanity in their writing in her creative writing class, NCTE wrote letters and gave testimony to defend Lacks and the freedom of students to write. Lacks, who continues as an advocate for students' right to write and for teachers, was recognized with many awards, including the NCTE National Intellectual Freedom Award.

- When the state of Virginia tried to insist that teachers label the texts they were teaching with ratings according to sexual content, NCTE wrote statements on the state school board's public comment website and letters to legislators and to the governor. We worked with NCTE's Virginia affiliate to have members send letters of protest to their legislators on more than one occasion. NCTE and VATE members visited gubernatorial staff. There were newspaper op-eds, interviews, and public statements. The proposed rating scheme failed.

Many other challenges have remained private because the challenge was between the teacher and the school district.

It would be great if our discussions with parents could be conducted as the kind of meta-moments (Petrone, 2015) Horner describes in this book. We could listen to parents carefully and attentively, then ask them to think a moment, take the high view, and state what their feelings are about the text and their student reading it. No promises here, but it is worth a try. And, if parents believe they still must challenge the text, we could offer their students an alternative text. Better yet, we might have all students work in groups, each with a different text, with some texts being safer than others to potential challengers.

Often challengers react to parts of a text (an incident on a certain page of the book—such as the boys-on-boy rape scene early in *Kite Runner*); to something they don't approve of and don't want their student or any student to read about (such as sexuality in *A Bad Boy Can Be Good for a Girl* or *Beloved* or *Looking for Alaska*, or magic in the Harry Potter books); or to something they've seen in a movie about the book (Atticus Finch as white savior in the film version of *To Kill a Mockingbird* versus Scout as questioner of the adult behaviors she sees in the book version); or to language in the text (like the use of the N-word in *The Adventures of Huckleberry Finn* or Lenny's talk in *Of Mice and Men*). It's very important to remind challengers that we teach whole texts and not bowdlerized parts, that their students are likely way stronger and wiser than they give them credit for being, and that students need and benefit from books that parents often object to (such as *Eleanor & Park* and *The Hate U Give*). In addition, we often teach controversial materials. In fact, the Supreme Court case *Island Trees Union Free School District v. Pico* (1982), which NCTE joined in amicus curiae, established that minors do have First Amendment rights in schools, including the right to receive information, even controversial information. This means that a text used in class need not agree with the challenger's beliefs (for example, *Persepolis*, *Mexican WhiteBoy*, *Two Boys Kissing*, and *The New Jim Crow*) and that students can write on and discuss a wide variety of issues on which there is disagreement. Note the *Monteiro v. Tempe Union High School District* decision recognizing the First Amendment right of students to read books selected for their "legitimate educational value" (1988), even if offensive to some parents and students. The blog *The Post, the First Amendment, and the Student Press* (Davis, 2018) focuses on an earlier US Supreme Court decision governing student publications (*Hazelwood v. Kuhlmeier*, 1988) that gives principals the right to censor those publications if they fear the publication will cause disruption in the school or community. NCTE has joined student press organizations in the New Voices Initiative to get states to remove the restrictions of *Hazelwood*. Note that the body of law pertaining to student writing is much less defined than that pertaining to students' right to information. Although the *Hazelwood* ruling speaks to student publications, there are no established rulings on student writing in class. Most states and districts do have rules requiring teachers to report students whose writing is disturbing or threatening.

Despite our efforts, challenges may happen. The first step is to keep your head. Then contact the NCTE Intellectual Freedom Center (http://www2.ncte. org/resources/ncte-intellectual-freedom-center/), where you can explain the situation and be heard, ask questions, receive resources, and walk through some possibilities for handling the challenge.

Sometimes we'll want to involve other organizations, including the following:

- National Coalition Against Censorship (NCAC) (http://ncac.org/report-censorship-page). NCTE is a member of the coalition. According to the mission statement, NCAC supports the "freedom to explore, the freedom to think, the freedom to create," and through the Kids' Right to Read Center deals with a wide variety of challenges to classroom materials and to student rights. Most challenges result in a letter to the school board—NCTE is often a signatory on these. NCAC also deals with other sorts of challenges, such as the display of artwork in a wide variety of venues and more. They have staff with legal expertise.

- American Library Association (ALA) (http://www.ala.org/aboutala/offices/ oif). ALA's Office of Intellectual Freedom focuses on challenges to libraries in schools or communities. It produces the annual list of most challenged books and was the initiator of Banned Books Week (http://www.banned booksweek.org/ where you can also find resources). It has staff with legal expertise and a nationwide network of librarians who report on challenges in their areas. NCTE works with ALA on library challenges, and ALA occasionally signs onto NCAC letters.

- Comic Book Legal Defense Fund (CBLDF) (http://cbldf.org/resources/). CBLDF supports intellectual freedom by making various resources available, specifically working with challenges to comics or graphic novels, and by signing onto letters produced by NCAC. CBLDF is a great resource for information about graphic novels.

- Your local teachers' union can help you should the challenge arise to a personnel issue such as suspension or insubordination.
- American Civil Liberties Union (ACLU) (https://www.aclu.org/defending-our-rights). The ACLU is a great organization to have on your side if you think your civil liberties have been tampered with. NCTE and NCAC have worked with ACLU in challenge cases that have become political. ACLU staff are quite knowledgeable about personal freedoms and local and state education politics.
- American Booksellers for Free Expression (http://www.bookweb.org/abfe) is a great supporter of free expression in books. They are often signatories on the letters NCAC sends.
- Authors Guild (https://www.authorsguild.org/) supports working writers and their works. Authors Guild writes letters in defense of authors' books and often signs onto letters that NCAC sends.
- Society of Children's Book Writers and Illustrators (SCBWI) (https://www.scbwi.org/) supports those individuals writing and illustrating for children and young adults in the fields of children's literature, magazines, film, television, and multimedia. SCBWI writes letters in support of children's book writers and illustrators, and is often a signatory on letters from NCAC.
- PEN America Children's and Young Adult Books Committee (https://pen.org/childrensyoung-adult-book-authors-committee/) supports writers and librarians whose books have been banned or challenged. The committee writes its own letters and commentaries and often signs onto letters from NCAC.

Helpful NCTE Position Statements and Resources

- *The Students' Right to Read* (http://www2.ncte.org/statement/righttoread guideline/)
- *NCTE Beliefs about the Students' Right to Write* (http://www2.ncte.org/statement/students-right-to-write/)
- *Guidelines for Selection of Materials in English Language Arts Programs* (http://www2.ncte.org/statement/material-selection-ela/)
- *Rationales for Classroom Texts* (http://www.ncte.org/action/anti-censorship/rationales)
- *Guidelines for Dealing with Censorship of Instructional Materials* (http://www2.ncte.org/statement/censorshipofnonprint/)
- *Statement on Classroom Libraries* (http://www2.ncte.org/statement/classroom-libraries/)

- *NCTE Position Statement Regarding Rating or "Red-Flagging" Books* (http://www2.ncte.org/statement/rating-books/)
- *NCTE Position Statement on Academic Freedom* (http://www2.ncte.org/statement/academic-freedom/)
- *Statement on Censorship and Professional Guidelines* (http://www2.ncte.org/statement/censorshipprofguide/)

References

Buehler, J. (2016). Being proactive: Helping others understand YA lit and YA pedagogy. In Buehler, J., *Teaching reading with YA literature: Complex texts, complex lives* (pp. 121–54). Urbana, IL: NCTE.

Davis, M. (2018, February 14). The post, the first amendment, and the student press. [Blog post]. Retrieved from http://www2.ncte.org/blog/2018/02/post-first-amendment-press/

Kaplan, J. (2016, October 26). The censors are coming: what you need to know [Blog post]. NCTE, National Council of Teachers of English. Retrieved from http://www2.ncte.org/blog/2016/10/censors-coming-need-know/

Kittle, P. (n.d.). Letter to parents about reading and writing. Retrieved from http://pennykittle.net/index.php?page=resources

Knox, E. (2015). *Book Banning in 21st-Century America*. Lanham, MD: Rowman & Littlefield.

Monteiro v. Tempe Union High School District, US Court of Appeals 9th Circuit. (1998). Retrieved from https://caselaw.findlaw.com/us-9th-circuit/1281281.html

National Council of Teachers of English (NCTE). (2014, July 31). *NCTE beliefs about the students' right to write [SRW]* [Position Statement]. Retrieved from http://www2.ncte.org/statement/students-right-to-write/

National Council of Teachers of English (NCTE). (2018, October 25). *The students' right to read [SRW]* [Position Statement]. Retrieved from http://www2.ncte.org/statement/righttoreadguideline/

OurStory. (2017). Retrieved from http://www.diversebooks.org/ourstory/

Perrillo, J. (2018, September 29). More than the right to read. [Blog post]. Retrieved from http://www2.ncte.org/blog/2018/09/more-than-the-right-to-read-2/

Petrone, R. (2015, November). Learning as loss: Examining the affective dimensions to learning critical literacy. Paper presented at the NCTE Annual Convention, Minneapolis, MN.

We Need Diverse Books. (2019). Retrieved from https://diversebooks.org/

Chapter Ten

Adventurous Thinking: Provocative Curriculum and Pedagogy, Criticality, Community, and Connections

Mollie V. Blackburn

Throughout this book, you have met teachers from across the country engaging students in adventurous thinking, preparing students for the fights of their lives by promoting their rights to read and write texts that explore issues of equity and diversity. Just as the texts they read and write explore these issues, so too do the students who read and write them. These student explorations are guided by compassion, but also by the students' own strength and that of their teachers. Their explorations, with this guidance, draw on understandings of complexity and sophistication. The end goal of these explorations is not an "indoctrination of a certain set of beliefs and standards," but rather an "investigation of ideas" (NCTE, 2018, p. ix). As Vanderhule, who wrote compellingly in "High School Students' Rights to Read and Write as and about LGBTQ People," reflects on her teaching,

> I do not think that every student shared the same beliefs about the topics we discussed in those classes. I do not expect that to be true, but I witnessed students who were typically silenced speak out in the midst of a social climate that was telling them to be quiet. (this text, p. 76)

Thus, the end goal of this work that demonstrates the best of students' rights to read and write is not indoctrination, but preparation. In the words of Talebian, who, in "Black Lives Matter," underscored this critical point, "we prepare ourselves and our students to participate productively in movements aimed at achieving justice directly within our community" (this text, p. 46).

The young people you've met in these pages are preparing to work within and against their communities, composed of schools and governments, among other institutions. They are preparing to work against white supremacy, racism, xenophobia, homophobia, transphobia, and ableism. They are preparing to work on behalf of those who are minoritized because of their race, nations of origin, languages, religions, sexual identities, gender expressions, physical disabilities, mental illnesses, and homes, including but not limited to themselves. In learning about the Black Lives Matter movement, immigration, linguistic diversity, Muslim Americans, LGBTQ people, disabilities, and rural communities, these young people prepare to revolt against that which holds them back, holds them down. Teachers and readers who are already doing this work may recognize themselves in the approaches used by the featured teachers in this book; those who are new to this way of thinking may find mentors and models as they see how teachers in all sorts of classrooms are able to bravely support students' rights.

Pedagogical Expertise

We know that such preparation, though, depends not just on teachers' willingness to teach controversial content or texts, but also on teachers' expertise in teaching them. Pedagogical expertise includes broad understandings of what a given course might be or do, specific strategies in which particular content might be taken up with students, and even informal but deliberate moves to be made in regular interactions with students.

We see the importance of broad understandings of courses in Anderson's conceptualization of journalism and the way it

> gives students a reason to care about something outside themselves. It gives them permission to talk to people that they otherwise wouldn't. It teaches them how to listen. It teaches them how to record and tell the smaller stories that will one day make up our history. (this text, p. 20)

Anderson's expertise in teaching journalism with this understanding propelled her students to make powerful contributions to the discussion of immigration in the United States. We also see the significance of broad understandings of courses in the way that Ragozzino works so deliberately through her pedagogical expertise to make her curriculum accessible to all her students, with particular attention to and respect for those learning English. She understands this as her ethical responsibility and fulfills it.

Such broad understandings, though, come to life via specific pedagogical strategies. Horner, for example, points to the usefulness of meta-moments (Petrone, 2015) to help students work through their resistance to interrogate their privileges. Talebian examines the value of personal narratives, both the reading and writing of them, as students move toward plans of action. Similarly, Rahman points to vicarious learning and autoethnography as noteworthy ways to "expel one misconception, one stereotype, and one injustice at a time" (this text, p. 40). All of these specific strategies are ones that can be tried out, played around with, and modified for use in a wide array of secondary ELA classrooms.

There are also the more informal aspects of pedagogy that still demand expertise. Vanderhule, for example, talks about the impact she has on her students merely in the way she introduces herself to them. Similarly, Talebian and Anderson assert the power of framing the issues, in Talebian's words, or setting the stage, in Anderson's words. Blair's questioning can also be understood as an informal pedagogical move. By asking students questions not only about disability, both physical and mental, but also about how disability is a part of their lives, "the literature became less an artifact of the past and more an invitation to consider the present" (this text, p. 87). As we see pedagogical expertise in these models of broad understandings of courses, specific strategies, and informal approaches to engaging students in adventurous thinking, we can imagine how they might take shape in our own secondary ELA classrooms.

Undergirding Values

Undergirding these text themes and pedagogical approaches are a collection of shared values: criticality, community, and connection. These values run through the entire book.

Criticality. Criticality is the recognition, interrogation, and dismantling of inequitable power dynamics defined in any number of ways, including but not limited to race, nationality, language, religion, sexuality, ability, and region. That said, it is not the recognition, interrogation, and dismantling of just any inequitable power dynamics; rather, the power dynamics of interest to those taking a critical approach are the ones that are institutionally reified. In this book, we see examples of teachers critiquing biases against their students, teachers guiding their students to be critical of biases that work against them, and teachers guiding their students to recognize biases that they might have against others and to interrogate and dismantle these biases.

We get a clear example of teachers recognizing, interrogating, and dismantling inequitable power dynamics that negatively impact their students in Ragozzino's account. She examines linguistic diversity and focuses specifically on English-only policies and practices. She reflects on the damage these do and counters this damage by asserting that "what [her] students bring to [her] classroom, with their rich and varied cultural backgrounds, experiences, and knowledge, enriches and enhances any textbook lesson that I could ever offer" (this text, p. 31). In doing so, Ragozzino works as an advocate for her students.

Talebian, however, really provoked her students to advocate for themselves against the racism they experience. She guided her students to recognize and interrogate institutional and lethal racism, for example, by studying and composing personal narratives, among other texts. She actively claims that the ELA classroom "must interrogate acts of physical and linguistic violence against Black and Brown youth and take them into consideration when shaping curricula" (this text, p. 52). It is this sort of work that prepares students for dismantling the institutional systems that oppress them.

Anderson and Horner, though, challenged their students to recognize and interrogate the ways that others are oppressed. Anderson created contexts in which her students contested anti-immigration policies and practices by creating a context in which her journalism students researched and wrote, and thus came to know, the struggles of immigrant families in their communities. She quotes her student Kyndall as saying, "I think teachers should teach teenagers to be critical of the world around them and do everything that they can to find the truth around them" (this text, p. 15). Horner, on the other hand, worked through resistance as she guided her white and rural students to reflect on the role of race and racism in their world, their country, their community, and themselves.

These categories, of course, are not so neat and tidy. Rahman made it clear when she was working with Muslims to navigate Islamophobia in schools versus working with Catholics, for example, to understand the experiences of their Muslim peers. She writes,

> Taking [a critical literacy] approach in my own teaching and classroom allowed my students and me to connect with each other and with the texts we were reading in class in a way that opened doors to question why things are the way they are, and whether there are things in our lives that need further exploration in order to bring about change that will benefit us all. (this text, pp. 36–37)

The lines are even blurrier in Vanderhule's and Blair's accounts. Vanderhule invited students to trouble the power dynamics defined by gender and sexuality, by analyzing various representations of Mercutio, for example. While most of her students were cisgender and straight, not all of them were, and some of them seemed to ask themselves questions about these claimed identities as a result of their processes of analysis. Similarly, Blair's students began to ask themselves how disability is a part of their lives as they read, discussed, and wrote about physical disabilities and mental illness. Thus, criticality in secondary ELA teaching provoked both teachers and students to recognize, interrogate, and strive to dismantle inequitable power dynamics.

Community and connection. Just as criticality undergirds the work these teachers do, so too does community and connection. Some of these teachers focus on students working in and contributing to their communities. Talebian writes about students working in their communities. She states that the fighting, the loving, the reflection, the understanding, the transformation of power "begins right in our community" (this text, p. 52). Anderson talks about students contributing to their community. She writes,

> I want students to know and understand the people and issues in our community. I want students to put faces on significant topics such as immigration. I want students to use words responsibly to capture life, to inform our communities, to inspire change, and to give hope. (this text, p. 20)

Ragozzino considers how both students and teachers have much to give their community. She says, "Welcoming linguistic diversity in our classrooms . . . will strengthen our classrooms, our schools, and our communities" (this text, p. 31). Even though there is much promise in students' communities, across this book there is also a profound awareness of the struggles of communities. Rahman acknowledges deep divides within communities, and her students inspire all of us to reach across them as they

> [analyze] the conflicts between the people belonging to the two faiths, how such issues [impact] the youth of these communities, and how friendship could potentially open doors for reconciliation, if not on a grand or global level, then perhaps on a local or societal level. (this text, p. 38)

In other words, the promise of communities is not squelched by struggles even if challenged by them.

Implicit in the discussion of communities is the discussion of connection. Blair explicitly values the connection made between himself and students as they explored experiences with disability. He says,

> As their honesty bears out, our students live with disability themselves. They know people who live with it. They recognize the presence of it around them. And I found myself connecting with them on a deeper level as I saw how much their experiences with disability echoed—and even enriched my personal understanding of—my own. (this text, p. 87)

Horner also values connections between herself and students while simultaneously appreciating connections with parents and even literature and life:

> Whether it's around a Montana bonfire, on a city subway, or in an ELA classroom, when texts, conversations, and diverse ways of knowing begin to make previously invisible structures, policies, practices, and norms visible, students—and parents and faculty—have emotional reactions. . . .
>
>   . . . [T]he collective task then becomes about finding routes within the classroom to intersect, acknowledge, and expand the emotional literacy, via listening, talking, reading, writing, and understanding, of students and teachers—myself included—as a way to connect and step into literature and life more fully and deeply. (this text, pp. 65–66)

Connections are central to communities. Disconnections, too, are a part of communities, as communities are diverse and complicated.

Still, communities and connections within and among them matter. As Talebian states,

> Our classrooms matter. Healing and humanizing classrooms matter most. With the goal of helping our community interrupt chronic systems of oppression, our classrooms need to become spaces of healing where all of our literature and writing is innovative and designed to explore foundational issues that ground race, class, and ethnicity, thus creating a language of solidarity. (this text, p. 52)

Let me underscore: Healing. Humanizing. Solidarity.

All of this, it seems to me, prepares students for adventurous thinking: provocative curriculum and pedagogy, for sure, but also criticality, community, and connections.

Preparing to Stimulate Adventurous Thinking

Anderson warns, "If we don't start using our classrooms to foster student voices who use their First Amendment rights, then we are complacently participating in the quiet erosion of our democracy that starts within our classroom walls" (this text, p. 20). She goes on to challenge us:

> As teachers, we have an important choice to make and an essential job to do. It is up to us to let students know their rights and then to build our practice around supporting and protecting our students' rights to read and write. (this text, pp. 20–21)

This challenge is implicit in the quotation from which the title of this book, *Adventurous Thinking*, was derived. In it, Justice William O. Douglas, in reference to the 1952 US Supreme Court case *Adler v. Board of Education*, insists that social, cultural, and political problems must be "pursued with impunity to [their] edges" and that teachers must do their part in this effort by serving as "stimulant[s] to *adventurous thinking*" (epigraph to this book). It is *this* that this book strives to prepare *you* to do.

References

National Council of Teachers of English (NCTE). (2018, October 25). *The students' right to read* [*SRR*] [Position Statement]. Retrieved from http://www2.ncte.org/statement/ righttoreadguideline/

Petrone, R. (2015, November). Learning as loss: Examining the affective dimensions to learning critical literacy. Paper presented at the NCTE Annual Convention, Minneapolis, MN.

Annotated Bibliography

Blackburn, Mollie V., Caroline T. Clark, Lauren M. Kenney, and Jill M. Smith, eds.
Acting Out! Combating Homophobia through Teacher Activism.
New York: Teachers College Press, 2010.

This is an edited volume comprising teachers' accounts of their striving to be advocates for LGBTQ people in schools. Many of the chapters are written by high school English teachers and represent their efforts at including LGBTQ representation in their curriculum and running their schools' GSAs.

Blackburn, Mollie V., Caroline T. Clark, and Ryan Schey, with Jenell Igeleke Penn, Courtney Johnson, Jill Williams, Dorothy Sutton, Kim Swensen, and Lane Vanderhule
Stepping Up! Teachers Advocating for Sexual and Gender Diversity in Schools.
New York: Routledge, 2018.

This book draws on more than seventy interviews with stakeholders in schools, including teachers, students, parents, and administrators, in an effort to understand when and why people step up on behalf of LGBTQ people in schools and when and why they do not. It offers explicit guidance in how to make this work more doable.

"Developmental Disability News."
Disability Scoop. www.disabilityscoop.com/

In the site's own words, "Disability Scoop is the nation's largest news organization devoted to covering developmental disabilities." Whether teachers embark on a disability studies approach in their classrooms or not, they will still find this site informative and illuminating. It provides a wealth of articles about the many current issues dealing with disability that impact our students (and our society as a whole).

Duarte, Fernanda P.
"Using Autoethnography in the Scholarship of Teaching and Learning: Reflective Practices from 'the Other Side of the Mirror.'"
International Journal for the Scholarship of Teaching and Learning, 1(2), 1–11, 2007.

Autoethnography is a reflective writing practice that Elma Rahman began to incorporate in her everyday teaching because it gives both students and teachers the ability to gain new insights through narrative writing in which one examines issues and topics in relation to one's own experience. Fernanda P. Duarte focuses on the teacher perspective because it allows educators to rethink curriculum through implementation and ongoing inquiry.

Dunn, Patricia
"Disability-Themed YA Literature: Questioning Our Choices, Questioning Our Questions."
[Blog post, 2 Dec. 2015]. Retrieved from http://www.yawednesday.com/blog/disability-themed-ya-literature-questioning-our-choices-questioning-our-questions

In this post, Dunn makes a good case for how literature often tackles disability. It also brings up the problems of unspoken messages in a clear and accessible manner. In addition, it provides some great possibilities for texts that teachers could use. Blair actually first came across _Narrative Prosthesis_ when he read this piece, and Dunn does a wonderful job of presenting Mitchell and Snyder's position.

Dunn, Patricia

"Fictional Characters with Disabilities—What Message Do They Send?"

[Blog post, 29 Aug. 2016]. Retrieved from blogs.ncte.org/index.php/2016/08/fictional-characters-disabilities-message-send/

Patricia Dunn, who served for five years as the editor of the "Disabling Assumptions" column in *English Journal*, was extremely helpful to Blair in getting his head around the presence of disability in literature. She was gracious with her time and her expertise. This particular article, which Blair quotes liberally in his chapter, provides a great introduction to issues of stereotyping and to the thematic implications surrounding disability. Although Dunn's focus is on YA texts, her list of questions to consider in texts is applicable to all literature.

Freire, Paulo

Pedagogy of the Oppressed, 30th anniversary ed.

New York: Continuum, 2005.

"To the oppressed, and to those who suffer with them and fight at their side." This text is a grounding piece of work that allows educators to grasp the humanizing force of education as a practice for liberation. It underscores the importance of identifying oppressor and oppressed like dynamics that exist in classrooms. Building on this idea, Freire deconstructs oppression in the classroom while rebuilding it with notions of love and hope.

GLSEN

www.glsen.org

This site offers professional development resources as well as classroom resources to enhance and create a more inclusive classroom environment. It is also a valuable resource for educators who are interested in starting a GSA in their school.

Gorski, Paul C.

"Cognitive Dissonance: A Critical Tool in Social Justice Teaching."

Retrieved from http://www.edchange.com (2009).

In his article, Gorski shares his experiences of explicitly teaching about cognitive dissonance as a way to delve more deeply into issues of social justice in the classroom. Teachers interested in bringing issues of social justice into the classroom might read this article to gain another pedagogical tool to use at the intersection of the ways in which students and teachers have been socialized to understand certain concepts and topics, and what might occur in a learning environment when new (often contradictory) information enters.

Hawthorne, Nathaniel

"The Minister's Black Veil."

(Original source *Mosses from an Old Manse*, vol. 1. New York: Wiley & Putnam, 1846.) Retrieved from http://andromeda.rutgers.edu/~jlynch/Texts/ministersblackveil.html

Nathaniel Hawthorne's short story paved the way for a lot of the work Rahman wanted to accomplish regarding getting students to examine similarities and differences in cultures and belief systems. It is a text that is an exemplar of American literature, easily aligned with Common Core State Standards, and complicated enough to do the kind of social justice work that allows students and teachers to be critical of dogmas and power systems through meaningful classroom discussion.

Kirkland, David E.

A Search Past Silence: The Literacy of Young Black Men.

New York: Teachers College Press, 2013.

Written in beautiful poetic narrative, Kirkland delves into the lives of six young Black males who have been overlooked as writers, poets, students, and activists. As we work to understand the complexities that young people of color face, as we revise curriculum daily to respond to them, Kirkland sets the case for the powerful role educators play in the process.

Kittle, Penny
Book Love Foundation.
Retrieved from http://booklovefoundation.org/ (2017).

Based on Kittle's *Book Love* (2012), this site offers practical advice on how to add independent novels to the classroom. It also provides a beautifully curated list of resources that support the benefits of choice reading in the classroom.

Lau v. Nichols
[Court case] 414 U.S. 563 US Supreme Court 1974.
Retrieved from https://en.wikipedia.org/wiki/Lau_v._Nichols

The 1974 *Lau v. Nichols* Supreme Court ruling states, "There is no equality of treatment merely by providing students with the same facilities, textbooks, teachers and curriculum for students who do not understand English [and therefore] are effectively foreclosed from meaningful education. . . ."

Mitchell, David T., and Sharon L. Snyder
Narrative Prosthesis: Disability and the Dependencies of Discourse.
Ann Arbor: University of Michigan Press, 2018.

Mitchell and Snyder's *Narrative Prosthesis* is another text Blair references in his chapter. Their second chapter, titled "Narrative Prosthesis and the Materiality of Metaphor," is especially rich in unpacking how disability is frequently treated in literature. University of Pennsylvania has a PDF of the full chapter; see https://www.english.upenn.edu/sites/www.english.upenn.edu/files/Mitchell-Snyder_Narrative-Prosthesis_Chpt2.pdf.

National Scholastic Press Association
http://studentpress.org/nspa/

The National Scholastic Press Association is another essential website for connecting teachers with other teachers who advise student publications. It is a great resource to see which students are being recognized across the country for their brave work. In addition to showcasing student work, there is an incredible Info Hub on the site. It includes links: Government Resources, Organizations, Technical Resources, Downloadable PDFs, and much more. This site also provides excellent models of student work.

Student Press Law Center (SPLC)
www.splc.org

The Student Press Law Center was essential when Anderson started her work, and it is still essential nearly twenty years later. SPLC provides free legal advice to any student, so we always know what our rights are, thanks to them. There is a For Classrooms tab on the SPLC homepage. It leads to story ideas, quizzes, presentations, and handouts. The SPLC focuses on press freedom and censorship, school transparency, civic participation, and online citizenship. The center has helped students across the country to confidently exercise their rights to read and write. This site and organization are must-haves for teachers who are embarking on this brave work.

Tatum, Beverly Daniel
"Talking about Race, Learning about Racism: The Application of Racial Identity Development Theory in the Classroom."
Harvard Educational Review, 62(1), 1–24, 1992.

In this article, Tatum discusses her experiences teaching about race, racism, and the myth of meritocracy—among other topics—in primarily white college classrooms, and the student resistance and emotionality that emerged as a result. This article is ideal for educators with a desire to learn more about including topics of race and racism in their curriculum as well as a framework for how to proceed when inevitable emotions and resistance become apparent.

Index

Editor

Mollie V. Blackburn is a professor in the Department of Teaching and Learning at the Ohio State University. Her research focuses on literacy, language, and social change, with particular attention to lesbian, gay, bisexual, transgender, queer, and questioning (LGBTQ) youth and the teachers who serve them. She is the author of *Interrupting Hate: Homophobia in Schools and What Literacy Can Do about It*, a coauthor of *Stepping Up! Teachers Advocating for Sexual and Gender Diversity in Schools*, and a coeditor of *Acting Out! Combating Homophobia through Teacher Activism*. She has received WILLA's Inglis Award for her work in the areas of gender, sexuality, sexual orientation, and young people; the Queer Studies special interest group of the AERA's award for a body of work; and the Alan C. Purves Award for an article in *Research in the Teaching of English* deemed rich with implications for classroom practice.

Contributors

Tracy Anderson has taught English in public schools for twenty-one years. She started at Pinckney High School and has worked at Community High School in Ann Arbor, Michigan, for the past eighteen years. She is the adviser for two state and national award-winning publications: *The Communicator Magazine* and *CHS Communicator Online*. She has co-authored two books, *Purposeful Writing* and *They Still Can't Spell?*, as well as articles in *English Journal*.

Jeff Blair teaches literature and writing courses at Grandview High School in Colorado. He is also an adjunct instructor for Community College of Aurora.

Millie Davis directs the Intellectual Freedom Center of NCTE, supporting literacy teachers across the country to ensure their students' right to know and learn, to read and write.

Melissa Horner teaches English at Park City High School in Park City, Montana. Her teaching and research focus on social justice, particularly as it involves teaching about issues of race and racism in a white, rural context.

Cat Ragozzino is currently teaching English to Speakers of Other Languages (ESOL) in grades 6 through 8 in Meriden, Connecticut. She has been teaching for thirteen years in urban communities as a secondary English teacher, a sheltered English teacher, and a teacher of ESOL. Additionally, she is on a team of ESOL teachers who train and coach teachers throughout the district in Sheltered Instruction Observational Protocol (SIOP) and adding instructional supports to the existing curricula to meet the needs of English Learners.

Elma Rahman currently works at the middle level for the New York City Department of Education as a seventh-grade ELA and humanities teacher. Previously, she taught in an Islamic private school.

Arianna Talebian is an inclusive ELA and social justice educator in Brooklyn, New York. Her passion and her development of a critically aware and transformative English education pedagogy have created a space where young people can engage and participate in movements aimed at achieving justice, and can participate in critical thinking and communication relating to social injustices.

Angie Thomas is the author of *The Hate U Give* and *On the Come Up*, the former of which was a number one *New York Times* bestseller and major motion picture from Fox 2000. Thomas was an inaugural winner of the Walter Dean Myers Grant in 2015. She earned her BFA in creative writing from Belhaven University.

Lane Vanderhule is a sixth-year teacher at Hilliard Davidson High School (Ohio), where she teaches general and AP English from a social justice perspective and works to create a culturally diverse and inclusive environment in her classroom. She advises the school's Gender and Sexuality Alliance (GSA) and the Intersectional Feminist Club and creates and provides LGBTQ-related professional development sessions for her colleagues throughout the Hilliard City Schools. Additionally, Lane is a nationally certified Professional Development Facilitator with GLSEN Columbus.

This book was typeset in Janson Text and BotonBQ by
Barbara Frazier.

Typefaces used on the cover include American Typewriter,
Frutiger, and Formata.

The book was printed on 50-lb. White Offset paper by
Seaway Printing.